TOUCHING THE EARTH

Touching the Earth

46 GUIDED MEDITATIONS FOR MINDFULNESS PRACTICE

Revised Edition

Thich Nhat Hanh

PARALLAX PRESS
BERKELEY, CALIFORNIA

Parallax Press
P.O. Box 7355
Berkeley, CA 94707
www.parallax.org

Parallax Press is the publishing division
of Unified Buddhist Church, Inc.

Cover design by Grégoire Vion.
Text design by Gopa & Ted 2, Inc.
Translated from Vietnamese by Sr. Annabel Laity.

Library of Congress Cataloging-in-Publication Data

Nhât Hanh, Thích.
  Touching the earth : guided meditations for mindfulness
practice / Thich Nhat Hanh. — Rev. ed.
      p. cm.
  Previously published: 2004.
  ISBN 978-1-888375-87-9
  1. Buddhist meditations. I. Title.
  BQ9800.T5392N45483 2008
  294.3'4432—dc22

                                        2007045371

1 2 3 4 5 / 12 11 10 09 08

Table of Contents

INTRODUCTION:
THE PRACTICE OF BEGINNING ANEW

At the foot of the mountain
there is a stream.
Take the water from the stream and wash yourself,
and you will be cured.

THESE WORDS ARE TAKEN from a well-known Beginning Anew ceremony traditionally used in Vietnam.* "Beginning Anew" comes
from the Chinese words *chan hui*. It means expressing our regret for
mistakes we have made in the past coupled with a deep and transforming determination to act differently from now on. Because we
know that we can act differently, we do not need to feel guilt.

To practice Beginning Anew is to bathe in the water of compassion.
Compassion gives us a chance to return to the joy of being alive. Once
the mind is concentrated on loving kindness and compassion, their
energy is produced and strengthened. When the nectar of compassion
flows in your heart, you can see clearly how to put an end to all your
afflictions.

The Beginning Anew practice described in this book is based on

---

* This is the source of Beginning Anew liturgy that was composed by Master Zhi Xuan, also
known as the National Teacher Wu Da, who lived from 811–883 C.E. in the Tang era in China.
This work is generally called Beginning Anew by Means of Water or Beginning Anew by
Means of Compassion, or the Samadhi of Compassion to Begin Anew by Means of Water.

the compassion of the earth. When we touch the earth, we take refuge in it. We receive its solid and inclusive energy. The earth embraces us and helps us transform our ignorance, suffering, and despair. Wherever we are, we can be in touch with the earth. Wherever we are, we can bow down to receive its energy of stability and fearlessness. As we touch the earth, we can follow our breathing. We release all our instability, fear, anxiety, disease, and anger. We know the earth can absorb our negativity without reacting to us or judging us. In this way, we're able to transform those things within us which are painful and difficult to accept. We're able to strengthen our capacity to look, speak, and act with understanding and compassion towards ourselves, our loved ones, and all members of our society. Touching the earth communicates our gratitude, joy, and acceptance to our Mother Earth. With this practice, we cultivate a relationship with the earth and, in doing so, we restore our balance, our wholeness, and our peace.

The preface to the Kshitigarbha Sutra says: "Earth means that which is stable, thick, and has a great capacity for embracing." The energy of mindfulness and concentration produced by touching the earth has the capacity to awaken us to the nature of reality, to transform us, to purify us, and to restore joy and vitality in our life. As soon as we begin to practice, we can taste the benefits. And the feeling of being at peace, refreshed and revitalized by the earth will continue long after our sessions of practice.

How to Use This Book

Each of the meditations in this book is a small conversation with the Buddha. Everyone can benefit from them and find a part that speaks to his or her own experience.

We can practice touching the earth by ourselves or with others. When we practice with others, one person can read the Earth Touching and everyone else can listen. It works well to rotate who reads. After one guided meditation has been read, everyone can touch the earth by lying down in the prostrate position or in the child's pose (kneeling and bending forward so that your forehead and forearms touch the ground). People unable to prostrate fully can simply join their palms and bow slightly. Touch the earth in silence and stay in that position for three long in–and–out breaths or longer. When practicing as a group, people sometimes choose to say "we" and "ourselves" instead of "I" and "myself" wherever it occurs in the meditation.

The meditations in this book are written to address the real concerns and difficulties found within a fourfold community of practitioners, which includes monks, nuns, laymen, and laywomen. What connects us all is our deep aspiration to live an awakened life in peace and harmony with ourselves and with others; our desire to heal the wounds that lie buried within our bodies and minds; and our commitment to serve society.

Certain parts of the meditations are addressed to monks and nuns while other sections are addressed to lay practitioners. Whichever we are, it may seem at first that some sections of the meditations don't apply directly to our present situation. Yet, looking deeply, we can find a way to relate to each section of the text. Whether we are practicing alone or as a community, these guided meditations can help us to slowly heal the divisions and uneasiness that we hold within us. A few days after a session of practice, perhaps hold a discussion with other practitioners to share the experiences and insights that arise.

If we enjoy this practice, we can do it as a daily practice, perhaps choosing a different meditation each day. Once every few months, try practicing one of the ceremonies at the back of the book. Try practicing all three ceremonies once or twice a year. Practicing Beginning Anew by Touching the Earth, we will find a feeling of joy rising up in us. Our difficulties will be transformed and our body and mind will grow lighter. The earth is present everywhere, and when we are in touch with it we can be at peace.

GUIDED MEDITATIONS
FOR TOUCHING THE EARTH

THESE MEDITATIONS are to be read as you stand or sit comfortably with palms joined. If you prefer, you can lie down on the earth during the reading instead. After each meditation, you can invite the bell and then bow down to touch the earth. Each meditation can be done on its own or as part of the Touching the Earth ceremonies for Beginning Anew. You do not need to do them in order! In fact, if you are new to the Touching the Earth ceremonies, perhaps begin with guided meditation number seven, Living in the Present, and then read through the others to find the ones that resonate with you.

1. Visualizing the World-Honored Buddha

Lord Buddha, I practice to be in touch with you as I touch the earth. I visualize you as a young man in Kapilavastu. I see you as an ascetic meditating in the wild mountains. I see you as a monk practicing samadhi solidly at the foot of the bodhi tree. I visualize you as a noble teacher instructing disciples on the Vulture Peak and in the Jeta Grove. I see you as a wandering monk whose mindful steps left their mark in the small kingdoms that lay in the valley of the Ganges River. Lord Buddha, you were healthy and strong in body and mind, living a long life without the help of modern medicines. I see you, my teacher, at eighty years old lying in the lion pose between the two sala trees before passing into nirvana. I touch the earth before King Suddhodana and Queen Maya, the two people who gave birth to Shakyamuni, offering this wonderful teacher to the world.

Touching the Earth

Buddha Shakyamuni, with body, speech, and mind united, I touch the earth in sincere gratitude to you, my root teacher, who manifested on this earth. [Bell]

Lord Buddha, I touch the earth in gratitude to your father, the King Suddhodana and your mother, the Queen Maya. [Bell]

2. The Buddha and the Original Sangha

Lord Buddha, I see you sitting with your Sangha of monks, nuns, laymen, and laywomen. I am like King Prasenajit who, whenever he saw the Sangha body of monks and nuns, felt how great you were and was filled with faith, respect, and admiration. I see your presence in the Sangha. You transmitted your wisdom and compassion to countless people. Lord Buddha, all of your disciples, whether monks, nuns, or lay practitioners, are in one way or another your continuation; they are the Buddha. I see you in the methods of practice you taught which, when used intelligently, always lead to transformation and healing. Lord Buddha, I recognize you in the energy of understanding and compassion embodied in people, in writings, poetry, architecture, music, and other works of art and forms of culture. I recognize you, the Buddha, in myself, in the seeds of awakening and love in me that make it possible for me to practice understanding and compassion.

Touching the Earth

Lord Buddha, with body, speech, and mind united, I touch the earth to be in touch with the Awakened One in myself, in the Sangha, in the teachings and practices of the Dharma, and in the wonderful opportunities that you have created for my spiritual life. [Bell]

With body, speech, and mind united in gratitude, I touch the earth before Buddha Dipankara, who predicted full enlightenment for my own root teacher, the Buddha. [Bell]

3. Outer Forms

Lord Buddha, I feel ashamed, because I have often practiced only the outer form, without any substance. While lighting incense, touching the earth, practicing sitting and walking meditation, or reading a sutra, I have allowed my mind to wander into the past and into the future, and I have caught myself in meaningless thinking about the present. I have lost many precious opportunities by not practicing deeply. While taking a mindful step or breathing mindfully, I have an opportunity to give rise to the energies of mindfulness and right concentration. When there is mindfulness and right concentration, the energies of awakening and understanding are always there.

I have been lucky enough to have been instructed in the practice. Yet, so often I am just like someone who knows nothing. I walk, stand, speak, and smile in forgetfulness. I promise, Lord Buddha, to do better so that in every moment of my daily life I give rise to more mindfulness and right concentration. Giving rise to mindfulness and concentration will not only help me to heal and transform body and mind, but will be a support to many other members of my Sangha body and will raise the quality of practice in the whole Sangha.

Touching the Earth

Lord Buddha, with body, speech, and mind in oneness, I touch the earth in gratitude to you, the one who has crossed wonderfully to the other shore and can show me the way, in order to remember the promise I have made. [Bell]

With body, speech, and mind in perfect oneness, I touch the earth in gratitude to Buddha Vipashyin. [Bell]

4. True Happiness

Lord Buddha, you and your Sangha are my teachers who have given me birth in the spiritual life and continue to nourish me every day. I am your disciple, your younger brother or sister, your son or daughter. I aspire to be your worthy continuation. You did not look for happiness in fame, wealth, sex, power, and luxurious food and possessions. Your great freedom, love, and understanding brought you happiness.

Thanks to your great understanding, you were not obstructed by your own mind or your surroundings and you were not caught in wrong thinking. You did not think, speak, or do things which would bring about suffering for yourself or others. Lord Buddha, thanks to this great understanding, you had limitless love for all species. This love comforted, liberated, and brought peace and joy to countless beings. Your great understanding and compassion gave you great freedom and happiness. My deepest desire is to follow in your footsteps. I vow that I shall not seek happiness in the five sense pleasures. I shall not think that wealth, fame, sex, power, and luxurious food and material objects can bring me true happiness. I know that if I run after these objects of craving, I shall incur great suffering and make myself a slave to these things. I vow not to run after a position, a diploma, power, money, or sex. I vow that every day I shall practice to give rise to understanding, love, and freedom. These elements have the capacity to bring true happiness for me and for the Sangha body now and in the future.

Touching the Earth

With body, speech, and mind in oneness, I touch the earth three times to experience and to solidify my deep aspiration. [Bell]

5. IMPERMANENCE AND INTERBEING

Lord Buddha, I wish to express my regret to you for my mistaken ways of thinking. Although I have learned of the impermanent nature of everything that is, and I myself may have spoken eloquently about it to others, I still have the habit of acting as if everything is permanent and I am a separate self. I am aware that my body is always changing. Every cell in my body will soon die and be replaced by a new cell. Still, I have the tendency to think that I am the exact same person today as I was yesterday. My five *skandhas*—body (form), feelings, perceptions, mental formations, and consciousness—are like five rivers that are constantly flowing, constantly changing. It is true that I can never bathe in the same river twice. I know that my feelings of anger or of joy will arise, stay for awhile, and eventually fade away to be replaced by another feeling. Yet I have the tendency to believe that my feelings, my perceptions, my mental formations, and my consciousness are permanent. I know that my belief in an unchanging, separate self, cut off from other people and living beings, has caused me to suffer and has caused others to suffer. Yet the deep, hidden tendency to be caught in the view of a separate self still lies in the depths of my consciousness.

I promise the Buddha that from now onwards when I am in touch with myself, when I am in touch with people and situations around me, I shall light up the awareness of interbeing and impermanence.

Intellectual knowledge that everything and everyone is interrelated and subject to change is not enough to transform my tendency to think that I am a separate self. I shall solidly practice to maintain the samadhi on interbeing and impermanence to nourish my awareness that all composed things are of the nature to change and that I am interconnected with all beings throughout space and time.

Gatha on Impermanence

The day has now ended.
Our lives are shorter.
Now we look carefully.
What have we done?

Noble Sangha, with all our heart,
let us be diligent,
engaging in the practice.
Let us live deeply,
free from afflictions,
aware of impermanence
so that life does not
drift away without meaning.

Touching the Earth

Lord Buddha, in gratitude I touch the earth three times to look deeply into and strengthen this vow I have made with you. [Bell]

6. Everything Is Manifestation

Lord Buddha, you have taught that people in the world are generally caught in ideas of being and nonbeing, permanence and annihilation. I know that the idea of an undying self is a wrong view, and I am practicing to look deeply to see that annihilation is also a wrong view. Permanence and annihilation are both extremes. You have taught me that if I am caught in either of these two extremes, I suffer. As part of my daily practice, I shall make an effort to see clearly that my own five skandhas and everything around me are impermanent, but at the same time are not subject to annihilation. With the clear understanding of impermanence, I see that nothing can be said to be a separate self-entity. Everything is a wonderful manifestation that does not have its own separate reality or its own separate nature. This manifests because that manifests, and that manifests because this manifests. This is present in that and that is present in this.

Lord Buddha, I shall listen to your advice and look deeply into impermanence, interdependence, emptiness, and interbeing in order to arrive at the deep realization that all that exists has the nature of no birth and no death, no coming and no going, no being and no nonbeing, no permanence and no annihilation. Lord Buddha, you have opened the door of no birth for us. I only need to follow you and enter that door. I know that the highest aim of a practitioner is to realize the nature of no birth and no death and thus to go beyond the cycle of samsara and attain the greatest freedom. You have been so compassionate to teach us this. Yet, I have wasted much precious time following a worldly career, looking for words of praise, profit, and position. I know I can do better.

Touching the Earth

Lord Buddha, with body, speech, and mind in perfect oneness, I touch the earth before you, the one who is truly and fully awakened, to express my regret for my unskillful and mistaken habits of thought. [Bell]

7. Living in the Present

Lord Buddha, I recognize my deep habit energy of forgetfulness. I often allow my mind to think about the past, so that I drown in sorrow and regret. This has caused me to lose so many opportunities to be in touch with the wonderful things of life present only in this moment. I know there are many of us whose past has become our prison. Our time is spent complaining or regretting what we have lost. This robs us of the opportunity to be in touch with the refreshing, beautiful, and wonderful things that could nourish and transform us in the present moment. We are not able to be in touch with the blue sky, the white clouds, the green willow, the yellow flowers, the sound of the wind in the pine trees, the sound of the running brook, the sound of the singing birds, and the sound of the laughing children in the early morning sunlight. We are also not able to be in touch with the wonderful things in our own selves.

We are unable to see that our two eyes are two precious jewels. When we open our eyes we can be in touch with the world of ten thousand different colors and forms. We do not recognize that our two ears are two wonderful sense organs. If we were to listen attentively with these two ears, we would hear the soft rustling of the wind in the branches of the pine, the twittering of the golden oriole, or the sound of the rising tide as it plays its compelling music on the seashore in the early morning. Our hearts, lungs, brains, as well as our capacity to feel, think, and observe are also wonders of life. The glass of clear water or golden orange juice in our hands is also a wonder of life. In spite of this I am often unable to be in touch with the way life is manifesting in the present moment, because I do not practice mindful breathing and mindful walking to return to the present moment.

Lord Buddha, please be my witness. I promise I shall practice to realize the teachings you have given us. I know that the Pure Land is not an illusory promise for the future. The Pure Land is available to me now, wonderful in all aspects. The path of red earth with its border of green grass is the Pure Land. The small golden and violet flowers are also the Pure Land. The babbling brook with small, shiny rocks lying in its bed is also the Pure Land. Our Pure Land is not only the fragrant lotuses and bunches of chrysanthemums, but is also the mud which nourishes the roots of the lotus and the manure which nourishes the chrysanthemums.

The Pure Land has the outer appearance of birth and death, but looking deeply I see that birth and death are interdependent. One is not possible without the other. If I look even more deeply, I will see that there is no birth and no death; there is only manifestation. I do not have to wait for this body to disintegrate in order to step into the Pure Land of the Buddha. By the way I look, walk, and breathe I can produce the energies of mindfulness and concentration, allowing me to enter the Pure Land and to experience all the miracles of life found right in the here and now.

Touching the Earth

Lord Buddha, I touch the earth twice to be deeply in touch with you and with the Pure Land of the present moment. [Bell]

8. Nourishing Love and Understanding

Lord Buddha, you have taught me not to regret the past or lose myself in anxiety and fear about the future. Around me I see many who are losing themselves in their worries and fears. This anxiety stops us from being able to dwell peacefully and live deeply in the present moment. I have the right and the ability to make plans for the future, but it is not necessary to lose myself in my worries about it. In reality, I know that the future is made of the present moment. When I live the present moment deeply and I only think, speak, and do what can bring more understanding, love, peace, harmony, and freedom into the present situation, then I have already done everything that I can to lay the foundation for a bright future.

The direction in which tomorrow's world will go and whether my descendants will have a chance to live happily and freely or not depends on how I live the present moment. To ensure a happy and peaceful future for my descendants I shall practice living simply, nourishing my heart and mind of understanding and love, and living in harmony with all those around me as true sisters and brothers in a spiritual family. If I continue to run after power, fame, riches, and authority I shall not have time to live peacefully and freely. I shall also continue to exploit unnecessarily the resources of our planet Earth, destroying the environment and bringing about strife and hatred in the world. This is not a positive way ahead for myself, for the environment, or for future generations. Lord Buddha, may I devote my life to nourishing a clear awareness of myself and my environment in every moment in order to continue your awakened way of looking and acting in the world. This is the noblest way of living.

Touching the Earth

Lord Buddha, with body, speech, and mind in perfect oneness, I touch the earth before you who has fully realized awakened understanding and action. [Bell]

9. CULTIVATING MINDFULNESS

LORD BUDDHA, according to your teachings, just returning to the present moment does not necessarily mean that I am able to dwell there with stability and freedom. I can be carried away by what is happening and lose myself. Mindfulness helps me to be aware when something is pulling me and taking away my stability and freedom. Sometimes I shun and sometimes I grasp at what is happening in the present moment. Both paths cause me to lose myself.

Practicing mindfulness, I can recognize what is happening in the present without grasping or aversion. I can practice mere recognition of what is going on within me and around me. This helps me to keep stability and freedom alive within myself. Lord Buddha, you have taught us that stability and freedom are two basic characteristics of nirvana. I vow that in my daily life I shall be more diligent in practicing mere recognition and mindfulness. I shall wash my hands with the awareness that I am washing my hands. I shall hold my bowl with the awareness that I am holding my bowl. When the mental formation of irritation arises I shall be aware that irritation is arising. When the mental formation of attachment arises I shall be aware that attachment is arising. I shall smile and recognize everything that is happening in the present moment without being anxious or having a complex, whether that complex is one of superiority, inferiority, or thinking myself just as good as the other.*

Touching the Earth

World-Honored Lord, I touch the earth before you, before the Buddha Kashyapa, and the Buddha Maitreya. [Bell]

---

* When we have the complex of equality we believe that we are just as good as others and we should be treated and regarded equally with others. But in reality each person has his or her characteristics, strengths, and weaknesses. For instance, a spiritual teacher upon understanding the nature of each student will treat him or her a bit differently according to the needs of that student, to best help that student to mature spiritually. To wish to be treated the same as everyone else can be an obstacle.

10. Healing Past Suffering

LORD BUDDHA, the past has left wounds in my body and mind. When I establish body and mind in the present moment I can still be in touch with the past. The mistakes I have made, the suffering I have caused in the past still leave their mark in me. I can recognize this suffering and smile at it.

I vow that from now on I shall be more skillful. I shall not think, speak, and act as I have done in the past. Lord Buddha, you have taught that thoughts come from the mind and thoughts are transformed by the mind. Once I have been able to recognize the marks of suffering left by the mistakes made in the past, I can vow not to repeat those mistakes again and the wounds in me begin to heal.

Repentance Gatha

All wrongdoing arises from the mind.
When the mind is purified, what trace of wrong is left?
After repentance, my heart is light like the white clouds
that have always floated over the ancient forest in freedom.

Touching the Earth

Lord Buddha, I touch the earth before you, the Awakened One whom people deeply respect and value, and before the bodhisattva Avalokiteshvara. [Bell]

11. Nourishing Our Ancestors and Descendants

Lord Buddha, in the Avatamsaka Sutra you have taught that the one contains the all and that the present contains not only the past but also the future. When I look deeply into the present, I can touch the future. I can be in touch with all my descendants because the future generations are already in me. I am aware that when I look after myself well in the present, I am looking after my descendants. When I have true love and compassion for myself, I have love and compassion for them. Whatever I offer myself, I offer them. One thing I can offer myself many times a day is the mindful steps which I make with solidity, peace, and freedom. Every step like that nourishes me, my ancestors in me, and all the generations of descendants which are present in me waiting to manifest.

Another gift I can offer is every mindful breath, which brings about peace and freedom. This gift brings joy and life to me, my ancestors, and my descendants in this present moment. When I eat, I also nourish the body and the spirit of my ancestors and descendants. When I practice sitting meditation, I nourish my ancestors and descendants spiritually. My deep desire is to devote every moment of my practice to nourishing my ancestors and descendants. I am aware that every step, every breath, every smile, every look made in mindfulness is an act of true love. I do not want to nourish myself with toxic foods, whether they are edible food, the food of sense impression, the food of intention, or the food of consciousness.* I vow that I shall not consume any products that are toxic, whether food, drink, books, magazines, films, music, or conversations. I do not want to nourish my ancestors and descendants with products that contain the toxins of craving, hatred, violence, and despair. I only want to nourish and offer to my ancestors and descendants wholesome foods that nourish, purify, and transform. I know that the practice of mindful consumption is the most effective way to protect myself, my ancestors, and my descendants. Consuming mindfully I express my deepest respect and love for myself, my ancestors, and all my descendants.

The only thing that I wish to transmit to my descendants, within me and outside of me, is the fruit of my daily practice—the energies of understanding and love. The only words and actions that I want to transmit to others are those that come from right view, right thinking, and right speech. I vow to live the present moment in such a way that I can guarantee a bright future for my descendants. I know that if my descendants are alive in me right now then I also will be alive in my descendants in the future.

Touching the Earth

Lord Buddha, I touch the earth before you who are fully enlightened, before the Bodhisattva of Great Understanding, Manjushri, and the Bodhisattva of Great Action, Samantabhadra. [Bell]

---

* The food of sense impression refers to what I consume with my six sense organs, namely my eyes, ears, nose, tongue, body, and mind, that is, I consume what I see, hear, smell, taste, feel, and think.

12. Living Deeply

Lord Buddha, by nourishing the awakened understanding of impermanence in me, I have understood clearly the Five Remembrances that you have taught us to meditate on every day.

1. *I am of the nature to grow old; there is no way I can escape growing old.*
2. *I am of the nature to have ill health; there is no way I can escape having ill health.*
3. *I am of the nature to die; there is no way I can escape death.*
4. *Everything that I cherish and value today I shall in the future have to be separated from.*
5. *My only true inheritance is the consequences of my actions of body, speech, and mind. My actions are the ground on which I stand.*

Thanks to nourishing the awareness of impermanence, I am able to cherish each day. World-Honored One, you knew how to use your time, health, and youth to lead a career of liberation and awakening. I am determined to follow your example, not running after power, position, fame, and profit. I no longer want to waste my time. I vow to use my time and energy to practice transforming my afflictions, giving rise to understanding and love. Lord Buddha, as your descendant and your continuation, I vow to practice so that your career of understanding and love can continue to live in all future generations of practitioners.

By nourishing the awareness of impermanence, I see the precious presence of the people I love: my parents, teachers, friends, and fellow practitioners. I know that my loved ones are as impermanent as I am. There are times when I am forgetful, and I imagine that my loved ones will be alongside me forever, or for as long as my life lasts. I think that they will never grow old, they will never be sick, and they will never be absent from me. I do not value their presence. I do not find joy and happiness in being with them. Instead I speak and behave unkindly. At times, I even have a secret wish that my loved ones would go far away from me when I feel irritated with them. I have made them suffer, I have made them sad and angry, because I have not known how to value them. I am aware that at times I may have treated my father, mother, brother, sister, teacher, Dharma brothers and sisters, or partner in these thoughtless, cold, and ungrateful ways.

Lord Buddha, with all my heart I express regret for these faults. I shall learn how to say things like: "Father, you are still alive with me and it makes me so happy." "Brother or sister, you are a solid presence alongside me. To have you in my life gives me much joy." "Mother, I am a very lucky person to have you in my life." "Sister or brother, you refresh me and make my life more beautiful." I vow to practice using loving speech, first of all towards those I love closely and after that towards everyone.

Touching the Earth

Lord Buddha, the teacher of gods and humans, please be my witness. [Bell]

Respected teacher of filial piety, Mahamaudgalyayana, please be my witness. [Bell]

Respected teacher who humbly hid his deep understanding, Rahula, please be my witness. [Bell]

13. RECOGNIZING FEELINGS
AND EMOTIONS

LORD BUDDHA, thanks to practicing mindful breathing and walking, I am aware of what is happening around me. I can recognize different mental formations as they arise. I know that the wounds of my ancestors and my parents, as well as wounds from my childhood until now, still lie deep in my consciousness. Sometimes painful feelings associated with sadness rise up in me and if I do not know how to recognize, embrace, and help them to calm down, I can say things and do things that cause division or a split in my family or my community. When I cause division around me I also feel divided in myself. Lord Buddha, I am determined to remember your teachings, to practice mindful breathing and walking and produce more positive energy in my daily life. I can use this energy to recognize the painful feelings in me and help them to calm down. I know that suppressing these feelings and emotions when they come up will only make the situation more difficult.

Lord Buddha, thanks to your teachings, I know that these feelings and emotions for the most part arise from narrow perceptions and incomplete understanding. I have wrong ideas about myself and other people. I have ideas about happiness and suffering that I cannot let go of. I have already made myself suffer a great deal because of my ideas. For example, I have the idea that happiness and suffering come from outside of myself and are not due to my own mind. My ways of looking, listening, understanding, and judging have made me suffer and have made my loved ones suffer. I know that by letting go of these ideas I will be happier and more peaceful in my body and mind. By letting go of my narrow ideas and wrong perceptions, my painful feelings and emotions will no longer have a basis to arise.

Lord Buddha, I know that I still have so many wrong perceptions that prevent me from seeing things as they really are. I promise that from now on I shall practice looking deeply to see that the majority of my suffering arises from my ideas and perceptions. I shall not blame others when I suffer, but shall return to myself and recognize the source of my suffering in my misperceptions and my lack of deep understanding. I shall practice looking deeply, letting go of wrong perceptions, and helping other people let go of their wrong perceptions so that they can also overcome their suffering.

Touching the Earth

Homage to the Bodhisattva of Great Understanding, Manjushri. [Bell]

Homage to the elder of Great Understanding, Shariputra. [Bell]

Homage to the elder who recorded the teachings, Ananda. [Bell]

14. Reestablishing Communication

Lord Buddha, since I have been able to return home to myself and recognize the root of my suffering in the realm of my perceptions, I no longer blame God or human beings for my suffering. I am able to listen to the suffering of others and help them recognize that the root of their suffering lies in their perceptions. I shall use the practice of deep and compassionate listening to increase my ability to understand and love people. I shall not blame them. I know that once I have understood people I am able to accept them and love them. Then I am able to use loving speech to help others see that their suffering has also arisen from the way they have of looking, understanding, and depending on their ideas and perceptions. When they are able to see that, they also will no longer blame and harbor resentment against others. On the contrary, they will be able to see that when they let go of their wrong perceptions they will be happy and free.

Lord Buddha, I have seen many people who have been able to resolve their internal formations by the practice of deep listening and loving speech. They have been able to let go of their misunderstandings, reestablish communication, and rediscover happiness.

Lord Buddha, I shall touch the earth three times to make the deep aspiration that from now on instead of blaming and accusing other people, I shall wholeheartedly practice loving speech and deep listening to reestablish communication.

Touching the Earth

Homage to the Buddha Konakamuni. [Bell]

Homage to the Bodhisattva of Deep Listening, Avalokiteshvara. [Bell]

Homage to the respected teacher of Great Filial Piety, Mahamaudgal-yayana. [Bell]

15. WALKING IN FREEDOM*

L ORD BUDDHA, in the past I have had a habit of walking as if someone were chasing me. I just wanted to arrive quickly and did not have stability and inner freedom while walking. Through walking meditation, I have transformed a great deal. However, my practice of walking meditation is still not yet solid and not every one of my steps is taken in mindfulness. I see many people around me who do not have the capacity to live joyfully and at ease in the present moment because they have not yet had the opportunity to practice walking meditation. Lord Buddha, you have shared with us that life is only possible in the present moment. I want each of my steps to contain the energy of solidity and freedom, bringing me back to the present moment. I vow that every one of my steps will help me to be deeply in touch with life and the wonders of life. I know that I am still alive; I still have two healthy feet, and to walk as a free person on this planet Earth is the true miracle.**

Dear Buddha, in former times you walked everywhere in freedom, sharing the teachings of love and understanding. Wherever you went

---

* For practitioners who use a wheelchair you can adjust the wording in this text to refer to "moving around in mindfulness" rather than "walking." Please be creative so that the practice is alive and appropriate to your situation.

** These words, "The miracle is to walk on the earth," are taken from the Records of Master Linji, our ancestral teacher from the ninth century in China.

you left traces of footsteps taken in peace, joy, and freedom. Wherever you walked became a sacred place. Lord Buddha, I too want to use your two feet to take steps of peace and happiness on all five continents. In our own time the Sangha of the Buddha is present in nearly every country, not only in Asia but also in Europe, Africa, North and South America, Australia, and Oceania. We are present everywhere and we vow that every day we shall practice walking meditation so that the whole of the planet becomes a sacred place. Lord Buddha, in the past you accepted this Earth as your Buddha land. I want to continue your career, bringing the teachings and the practices of mindful living, love, and understanding and transmitting them to friends on all continents. Lord Buddha, I promise you that together as a Sangha we shall practice mindful walking everywhere we go to express our love, respect, and care for our precious Earth.

I know that when I make steps with mindfulness, peace, and joy, the Pure Land manifests immediately; the Kingdom of God becomes available right away. All the wonders of life are available in this moment, including the budding leaves, the pebbles, the streams, the squirrels, the sound of birds, the breeze, the moon, and the sparkling stars in the midnight sky. Yet, because I have often been pushed and pulled in many directions as I walk, I have not always been able to touch these wonderful things of life. Looking deeply I see that there is no phenomenon that is not wonderful: the drop of dew, the blade of grass, the ray of sunlight, a cloud, or a flash of lightning. In the past I have wandered around like someone who has nothing to live for. I have discarded the present moment in my search for an illusory happiness in the future. Now, thanks to your teaching of dwelling happily in the present moment (*drsta dharma sukha viharin*), I have begun to wake up.

My mindful breathing and walking bring me back to the present, and in this moment I am able to experience the Pure Land of the Buddha, here and now.

I promise that from now on I shall practice so that every step I take will bring me back to the present moment, to life, and to my true home. I vow that whenever I take a step I shall be aware of my breathing and the wonderful contact between the sole of my foot and the surface of the earth. I shall not speak when I am walking. If I need to say something I shall stop, put all my heart into what I am saying or into listening to the other speaking. Once I have finished speaking or listening, I shall continue my mindful walking. If the person who is walking with me does not yet know this practice, I shall stand still and share it with him or her. While I am walking I shall be able to put all my heart into every step and nourish the Dharma happiness that will refresh and heal my body and mind.

Our True Heritage*

The cosmos is filled with precious gems.
I want to offer a handful of them to you this morning.
Each moment you are alive is a gem,
shining through and containing earth and sky,
water and clouds.

You only need to breathe lightly
for the miracles to be displayed.

* "Our True Heritage" by Thich Nhat Hanh can be found in *Call Me by My True Names* (Berkeley, CA: Parallax Press, 2000).

Suddenly you hear the birds singing,
the pines chanting;
you see the flowers blooming,
the blue sky,
the white clouds,
the smile and the marvelous look
of your beloved.

You, the richest person on Earth,
who has been going around begging for a living,
stop being the destitute child.
Come back and claim your true heritage.
We should enjoy our happiness
and offer it to everyone.
Cherish this very moment.
Let go of the river of suffering
and embrace life fully in your arms.

Lord Buddha, I promise that I shall organize my daily life so that whenever I need to go somewhere on foot I shall walk mindfully, whether the distance I need to go is near or far. I shall walk mindfully whenever I walk from my bedroom to the bathroom, from the kitchen to the toilet, from the ground floor to the top floor, from the door to the parking lot. In the forest, by the bank of the river, in the airport, or in the market, wherever I am I shall apply the practice of walking meditation.

I vow to produce and radiate the energy of ease, freedom, stability, peace, and joy wherever I go. Lord Buddha, I know I only need to walk with mindfulness and concentration and I can be as one with your original Sangha.

Dear Buddha, King Prasenajit said that whenever he saw the Sangha of the Buddha going somewhere in mindfulness, with solidity and freedom, he had great faith in the Buddha. I vow to do as the Original Sangha of the Buddha did, so that whoever happens to see me walking will feel respect and faith in the path of understanding and love.

Touching the Earth

Lord Buddha, I shall touch the earth to feel your energy, the energy of the bodhisattva Dharanimdhara, Earth Holder, and the bodhisattva Kshitigarbha, Earth Store. [Bell]

16. Mindful Walking

Lord Buddha, I feel warmth in my heart every time I am able to talk to and confide in you. I feel your presence in every cell of my body and know you are listening with compassion to everything I say. You walked on this planet Earth as a free person. I also want to walk on this planet Earth as a free person.

Around me are people who do not walk as free people. They only know how to run. They run into the future because they think that happiness cannot be found in the present moment. They are walking on the earth but their minds are up in the clouds. They walk like sleep-walkers, without knowing where they are going. I know I also have the habit to lose my peace and freedom as I walk.

Dear Buddha, I vow to follow your example and always walk as someone who is free and awake. I vow that in every step I take my feet will truly touch the earth and I shall be aware that I am walking on the ground of reality and not in a dream. Walking like that, I am in touch with everything that is wonderful and miraculous in the universe. I vow to walk in such a way that my feet will be able to impress on the earth the seal of freedom and peace. I know that steps taken like this have the capacity to heal my body and mind as well as the planet Earth itself.

When I practice walking meditation outside with the Sangha, I vow to be aware that it is a great happiness to walk with the Sangha. With each step, I am aware that I am not a solitary drop of water but am part of a larger river. With mindful breathing and steps, I shall produce the energy of mindfulness and concentration that contributes to the collective mindfulness of the Sangha. I shall open my body and mind so that the collective energy of our Sangha can enter me, protect me, and help me to gently flow along like a river, harmonizing myself with everything that is. I know that by entrusting my body and mind, as well as my painful feelings, to the Sangha that they may be embraced and healed. In this way I shall be nourished as I am practicing mindful walking with the Sangha and make significant transformation in my body and mind. In the meditation hall I shall open myself to the Sangha's energy as I practice slow walking meditation, taking one step for my in-breath and one step for my out-breath. I vow to walk in such a way that every step can nourish me and my Sangha with the energy of freedom and solidity.

Touching the Earth

Buddha Shakyamuni, I bow down before you, before the bodhisattva Dharanimdhara, Earth Holder, and before the bodhisattva Sadaparibhuta. [Bell]

17. Sitting Like the Buddha

Lord Buddha, I truly want to sit as you sat, with my posture still, solid, and powerful. As your disciple, I also want to have your composure. I have been taught to sit with my back upright and relaxed, my head a straight continuation of my spine without leaning forward or leaning backward, my two shoulders relaxed, and one hand placed lightly on top of the other. I feel both solid and relaxed in this position. I know that in my own time most people are too busy and very few have the opportunity to sit still with inner freedom. I vow that I shall practice sitting meditation in such a way that I experience happiness and freedom while sitting, whether I sit in the full lotus, the half lotus, or on a chair with my two feet placed flat on the earth. I shall sit as someone who has freedom. I shall sit in such a way that my body and my mind are calm and peaceful. With mindful breathing I shall adjust my posture, helping my body to be calm and at ease. With mindful breathing I shall recognize and help to calm down feelings and emotions. With mindful breathing I shall light up the awareness that I have all the conditions necessary to unite body and mind and to give rise to joy and happiness. With mindful breathing I shall look deeply into my perceptions and other mental formations when they manifest. I shall look deeply into their roots so that I can see where they have come from.

Lord Buddha, I shall not look at sitting meditation as an effort to constrain body and mind, or as a means of forcing myself to be or do something, or as a kind of hard labor that will bring happiness only in the future. I vow to practice sitting in such a way that I nourish myself with peace and joy while sitting. Many of my blood ancestors have never been able to taste the great happiness of mindful sitting and I vow to sit for those ancestors. I want to sit for my father, mother, brothers, and sisters who do not have the fortune to be able to practice sitting meditation. When I am nourished by my practice of sitting meditation, all my ancestors and relatives are also nourished. Every breath, every moment of looking deeply, every smile during the session of sitting meditation can become a gift for my ancestors, my descendants, and for myself. I want to remember to go to sleep early so that I can wake up when it is still dark and practice sitting meditation without feeling sleepy.

When I am eating, drinking tea, listening to a Dharma talk, or participating in Dharma discussion, I shall also practice sitting solidly and at ease. On the hill, on the beach, at the foot of a tree, on a rock, in the guest room, on the bus, in a demonstration against war, or in a fast for human rights, I shall also sit like this. I vow that I shall not sit in places of unwholesome activity, in places where there is gambling and drinking, in places where people are fighting, arguing, blaming, and judging others, except when I have made the deep vow to come to those places to rescue people.

Lord Buddha, I vow that I shall sit for you. Sitting with a deep serenity and solidity, I shall represent my spiritual teacher, who has given me birth in the spiritual life. I am aware that if everyone in the world has the capacity to sit still, then peace and happiness will surely come to this Earth.

Touching the Earth

Shakyamuni Buddha, I touch the earth before you and before the two elder brothers of your Sangha, the Venerable Shariputra and the Venerable Mahamaudgalyayana. [Bell]

18. Right Speech

Lord Buddha, during your life you devoted a great deal of time to teaching the Dharma to monks, nuns, laymen, and laywomen. Your words water the seeds of understanding in those who hear them and help them to let go of their wrong perceptions. Your words show people how to go in a positive direction. They console and comfort those who are distressed and give them the confidence and energy they need. There were times when people asked you questions and you sat perfectly still, smiled, and said not a word. You saw that for these people, noble silence was much more powerful and eloquent than words. As your disciple I want to be able to do as you did and only speak when it is necessary to speak, being silent when it is necessary to be silent. Lord Buddha, I promise you that from now on I shall practice saying less. I know that in the past I have said too much. I have said things that were not beneficial to me or to those who listened to me. I have also said things that have caused myself and others to suffer.

In the first Dharma talk you gave to the five monks in Deer Park, you mentioned the practice of Right Speech, one of the eight Right Practices that belong to the Noble Eightfold Path. My own practice of right speech is still very weak. I have spoken divisive words, which made communication difficult between myself and others because of my wrong perceptions, because my thinking is not mature or because I spoke out of anger, pride, and jealousy. I know that when communication becomes difficult or is completely cut off, I cannot be happy.

I vow that from now on, whenever the mental formations of irritation, pride, and jealousy arise in me, I shall return to my mindful breathing so I can recognize them. I shall practice noble silence and not react by saying something negative. When I am asked why I am not speaking I shall truthfully say that there is irritation, sadness, or jealousy in me and I am afraid that if I were to speak it would create division. I shall ask to be able to express myself at another time when my mind is more peaceful. I know that if I do so I shall be able to protect myself and the other person. I know that I should also not repress my emotions. Therefore I shall use mindful breathing to recognize and look after emotions, and to practice looking deeply into the root of my mental formations. If I practice like that I shall be able to calm down and transform the suffering that I am feeling.

I know that I have the right and the duty to let my loved ones know about my difficulties and my suffering. However, I shall practice to choose the appropriate time and place to speak, and will speak using only calm and loving speech. I shall not use words of blame, accusation, or condemnation. Instead, I shall only speak about my own difficulties and suffering so that the other person will have a chance to understand me better. When I am speaking I can help the other person let go of their wrong perceptions concerning me, and that will help both of us. I shall speak with the awareness that what I say may arise from my own wrong perceptions concerning myself and the other person. I shall ask the other person that if he or she sees elements of wrong perception in what I say, to skillfully point it out to me and offer me guidance.

Lord Buddha, I promise that I shall practice mindful speech so that the other person may understand me and themselves better, without blaming, criticizing, insulting, or conveying anger. When I am sharing about my suffering, the wounds in me may be touched and the mental formation of anger may begin to arise. I promise that whenever anger and irritation begin to show themselves I shall stop speaking and return to my breathing so I can recognize the anger and smile to it. I shall ask the permission of the person who is sitting and listening to me to stop speaking for a few minutes. When I see that I have returned to a state of equanimity, I shall continue to share. When the other person speaks, I shall listen deeply with an even and unprejudiced mind. While I am listening, if I recognize that what the other person is saying is not the truth, I shall not interrupt him. I shall continue to listen deeply and wholeheartedly to understand what has led the other person to this wrong perception. I shall try to see what I have done or said to make that person misunderstand me in such a way. In the days that follow, I shall use gentle and skillful speech and action to help the other person adjust their perception of me. When the other person has finished speaking, I shall join my palms and thank that person for sharing sincerely and openly with me. I shall contemplate deeply what the other person has said so that my understanding and capacity to live in harmony with him or her deepens day by day. I am aware that opening our hearts and minds to each other gradually, we will be able to release our misperceptions, judgments, and criticisms of each other. With the practice of skillful and loving speech, I will have the best opportunity to nourish love and understanding.

Touching the Earth

Lord Buddha, with body, speech, and mind in perfect oneness I touch the earth before you and before the Bodhisattva of Deep Listening, Avalokiteshvara. [Bell]

19. Listening Deeply

Lord Buddha, I know that I still need time to learn the practice of deep listening of the bodhisattva Avalokiteshvara. Although my intention to listen deeply is strong, if, while I am listening, the seed of self-criticism is watered in me, it becomes difficult. Perhaps the other person does not yet know how to practice loving speech. The words of the other person may contain blame, judgment, and accusation. This waters the seeds of anger, hurt, and self-criticism in me. When these seeds manifest in my mind consciousness I lose my capacity to listen deeply and I close myself off from the other person. Although I may not say anything, the other person has the feeling that they are talking to a wall.

Lord Buddha, you have shared with me that whenever the mental formations of irritation and anger arise, I can return to my mindful breathing. I breathe lightly and embrace these mental formations. I remind myself that I am here listening to this person so that he can have an opportunity to speak about his suffering. I can help relieve his suffering through the compassionate practice of listening deeply. Without compassion in my heart, I am not truly practicing deep listening.

If I am not successful at listening deeply, I shall apologize to the person who is speaking. I can say: "I am sorry, Brother. I am sorry, Sister. I am sorry, Mother or Father. Today I do not have enough peace of mind to listen to you deeply. May I ask to be able to continue listening to you tomorrow?" I promise that I will not allow myself to fall into the trap of practicing only with the outer form without any substance.

Touching the Earth

Lord Buddha, with body, speech, and mind in perfect oneness, I touch the earth three times to remember carefully my vow to practice deep listening. [Bell]

Lord Buddha, I express my regret to you, the Tathagata, for the times I have failed in my practice of listening deeply. I vow to practice better when I next have the occasion to listen deeply. [Bell]

20. MINDFUL SPEECH

LORD BUDDHA, in the past, out of foolishness, I have said things that were untrue. Maybe I have told these lies to conceal my weaknesses or to embellish the image people have of me. Sometimes I have told lies because I am afraid that people will criticize me. Sometimes I say these things that are untrue because I want to gain something, or I want to avoid being blamed, or I say them out of arrogance and jealousy. Sometimes I have lied because I wanted the person who is listening to me to dislike the person whom I dislike or of whom I am jealous.

Lord Buddha, when I remember the times I have lied, I feel ashamed and I want to express my regret to you.* I vow that from now on I shall not be foolish enough to tell lies like that again. I promise that I shall speak with understanding and love to resolve conflicts between myself and others. I shall speak in such a way as to bring about reconciliation between different members of my family, my Sangha, between different sectors of society, and different nations. I shall not say things that are discriminatory, whether they are racial, religious, or any other kind of discrimination. I shall practice speaking about what is wholesome, beautiful, kind, and positive and about the real difficulties and

---

* There are two different mental formations of shame in Buddhism. One is wholesome regret about past actions and determination to do better in the future and the other is shame that is held onto and becomes a guilt complex and an obstacle for us.

sufferings of the different members involved in a dispute to help both sides understand each other better. When they have understood each other, I shall help them to come together to practice reconciliation and mutual acceptance.

In the situation of a conflict, I vow that I shall not say one thing to one side and something else to the other side to cause them to hate each other and to grow further apart. If someone comes to me to complain about her suffering thinking it has been caused by another, I shall first practice listening deeply to help that person suffer less. If I recognize that there are misperceptions in what she is saying, I shall use skillful means to help her look more deeply into the situation. Using skillful means I shall also help her to see the source of suffering that lies in her own misperceptions. I shall tell her about the difficulties, sufferings, and positive qualities of the other person so that she will remember them and see the situation more clearly. I shall encourage her to approach the other person or group so that they can sit down together and reestablish communication. If necessary, I shall volunteer to support her and help her say everything she has not yet been able to say to the other person. I shall avoid making myself an ally with one person and opposing the other, which will cause disharmony and unhappiness in my family or community.

Touching the Earth

Lord Buddha, with body, speech, and mind in perfect oneness I touch the earth before you, who has come from suchness, before the Buddha Prabhutaratna, and the bodhisattva Kshitigarbha. [Bell]

21. Harmonious Speech

Lord Buddha, I promise I shall be careful not to say anything that could bring about disharmony, division, or a split in my practice community or in my family. Whenever I have difficulties with another member of my family or community, I shall find a way to clarify my misperceptions. I shall not go and complain about the other person to someone else. I do not want my own negative energy to influence other people and diminish their joy and energy. In the past I have been guilty of doing this. Today I want to recognize my faults. I vow that I shall not repeat the foolish mistakes that I made in the past.

Touching the Earth

Lord Buddha, I touch the earth before the Three Jewels—the Buddha, the Dharma, and the Sangha—to express my regret for speaking in a way that brings disharmony into my family or community. I place my head on the earth before you, the Buddha, before the Venerable Maha-maudgalyayana, and the Venerable Mahakaccayana. [Bell]

22. Expressing Gratitude

Lord Buddha, I vow to train myself to express gratitude in my daily interactions. I shall practice saying such things as:

+ "How good to hear your voice on the phone."
+ "How lucky I am to live in your presence, my teacher, and to be able to walk alongside you, receiving the solidity of your practice."
+ "I feel confident in the future of Buddhism when I see a younger sister like you who is intelligent, happy, and diligent."
+ "Mother, do you know that you have passed on to me so many virtuous qualities, talents, and examples of loving kindness?"
+ "My child, I have often been unskillful. There have been times when I have not been able to understand your difficulties and suffering and therefore I have spoken and done things that have made you suffer. I am really sorry and I ask your forgiveness. I promise that I will not continue this kind of unskillfulness. If you love me, please help me to put this promise into effect."
+ "I treasure so much the moments that I can live near you, my friend, teacher, parent, or child. I am very fortunate every day that I am able to enjoy the happiness of being together."
+ Lord Buddha, please allow me to express my gratitude and appreciation to you. If there were not the Buddha, if there were not the

wonderful Dharma that the Buddha has taught, if there were not the Sangha body that practices and preserves this wonderful Dharma, how could I experience spiritual happiness today? Without a doubt, in past lives I and my ancestors have sown good seeds and, as a result, in this life I have been able to meet the Tathagata and to receive the wonderful seeds of the true teachings offered by the Buddha. The understanding and compassion of the Buddha have ended in me so many worries, fears, and misunderstandings. Even if I had a hundred thousand lifetimes to show my gratitude for the grace of this understanding, it would not be possible for me to do so.

Touching the Earth

Dear Buddha, I touch the earth three times to express my deep gratitude to you. [Bell]

23. MINDFUL CONSUMPTION

LORD BUDDHA, I am very happy that I am able to be vegetarian or mostly vegetarian.* As a vegetarian, I am able to nourish compassion, which is the basis for a happy life. Looking around I see many animals who have to eat each other to stay alive. The spider has to eat the fly or the butterfly. The snake has to eat the frog. The bird has to eat the caterpillar or the fish. The cat has to eat the mouse. The tiger has to eat the deer. I feel very grateful that I am not forced to eat the flesh of other living beings.

I know that the plant species also want to live and do not want to die, but these feelings are very small compared with the feelings and fears of death of the human and animal species. I know that out of compassion, bodhisattvas never have the heart to eat the flesh of living species and I also want to live as a bodhisattva. Lord Buddha, in the Sutra on the Son's Flesh, you teach me to eat in mindfulness so

---

* In the Buddhist monastic tradition, meat is not eaten except under certain conditions when it is needed to save one's life or, such as in the time of the Buddha, when it was offered as almsfood with the condition that it was not expressly killed for monastics. In current times, we have access to a great variety of wholesome and nutritious vegetarian foods. Although it is required of monastic members of the Plum Village community to be a vegetarian, it is not a requirement for lay practitioners. Yet moving in the direction of mindful and compassionate living, we are all encouraged to eat a vegetarian or partially vegetarian diet.

that I may maintain and develop my compassion.* In this sutra, you have told your disciples that eating unmindfully is like eating the flesh of our own sons and daughters. When I eat the flesh of living beings, I am aware that it is like eating the flesh of my own small child.

In developed countries people eat a lot of meat and drink a lot of alcohol, which has a destructive influence on the body and mind. The production of meat and alcohol also uses a disproportionate amount of land and resources, thus directly contributing to poverty and hunger all over the world. Huge amounts of wheat, rice, corn, and barley are used to produce alcohol and feed animals to be sold for meat. Every day, more than 40,000 children in the world die because of a lack of sufficient, nutritious food. Lord Buddha, you have taught that if I drink alcohol and eat meat in this way, I am not being mindful of suffering and am not able to nourish compassion. If the 40,000 children who die every day in the world are not my own children and grandchildren, then whose children and grandchildren are they?

Lord Buddha, I have made the vow to be vegetarian and I feel peaceful and happy because of this. I know that vegetarian food can taste good and be wholesome at the same time. I am encouraged when I see that in our own time the number of people who are vegetarian is growing. There are many people who are vegetarian because they are aware that to be vegetarian is beneficial for spiritual, physical, and mental health. There are also people who are vegetarian because they want to nourish their compassion. I am happy when I see that there

* For commentary on this sutra, see Thich Nhat Hanh, *Path of Emancipation* (Berkeley, CA: Parallax Press, 2000), pp. 84–91.

are associations that are striving to protect animals by preserving their natural habitats or preventing people from using animals in harmful experiments.

Touching the Earth

Lord Buddha, with body, speech, and mind in perfect oneness, I touch the earth three times to nourish my awareness of the suffering of all species in the world and to help me to nourish my compassion. [Bell]

24. Eating Organically

Lord Buddha, in the past decade, I have seen more and more people become aware of the need to protect our environment. Many people are actively supporting local and organic farmers and sustainable ways of cultivating the land. In the last century, countless forests have been cut down to clear land for grazing animals. The excrement and urine produced in raising animals has seriously polluted our fresh water sources. The use of toxic chemicals in farming has harmed all species of living beings, the earth, the water, and the air. It is only because of the greed of human beings that our Earth has to bear all this destruction.

I vow that I shall eat and drink mindfully. I shall not eat meat or drink alcohol, and I shall strive to encourage and support wholesome agriculture so as to respect the life of living beings and the environment. In my garden at home or in my monastery, I shall practice cultivating the soil organically. When I go to the market I shall try to buy the vegetables and fruits that are cultivated organically and to support farmers who are producing organic food. I shall practice eating only what I need so I can have enough money to buy organically grown vegetables, grains, legumes, and fruits.

Touching the Earth

I shall touch the earth three times to express my regret to my mother, the Earth. Mother Earth has protected, nourished, and embraced me for so many lifetimes. Yet, out of carelessness, I have caused her so much harm. Lord Buddha and ancestral teachers, please be my witness as I touch the earth. [Bell]

25. EATING WITH GRATITUDE

Lord Buddha, whenever I sit down to a meal, I vow to be grateful. I know that the time of eating is also a time of meditation. When I am eating, not only am I nourished physically, but I am also nourished in my spirit. When I join my palms before a meal I follow my breathing to bring my mind and body together as one. And in this state of purity and awareness, I will look at the food on the table or in my bowl and I will meditate on the Five Contemplations:

1. *This food is the gift of the earth, the sky, numerous living beings, and much hard and loving work.*
2. *May we eat with mindfulness and gratitude so as to be worthy of receiving this food.*
3. *May we recognize and transform our unwholesome mental formations, especially our greed.*
4. *May we take only foods that nourish us and keep us healthy.*
5. *We accept this food so that we may nurture our sisterhood and brotherhood, build our Sangha, and nourish our ideal of serving living beings.*

Dear Buddha, as a layperson, I may go to work every day to earn money to buy food for myself and my family. Yet, I do not think that the food is my food, or has been produced by me. Looking into my bowl of rice, I see clearly that this food is the gift of the earth and the sky. I see the rice field, the vegetable garden, the sunshine, rain, manure, and the hard work of the farmer. I see the beautiful fields of golden wheat, the one who reaps the harvest, who threshes the grain, who makes the bread. I see the beans sown in the earth becoming the beanstalk. I see the apple orchard, the plum orchard, the tomato garden, and the workers who are cultivating these plants. I see the bees and butterflies going from flower to flower collecting pollen to make sweet honey for me to eat. I can see that every element of the cosmos has contributed to making this apple or this plum that I am holding in my hand or this leaf of steamed vegetable that I am dipping into the soy sauce. My heart is full of gratitude and happiness. When I am chewing the food I nourish my awareness and my happiness and I do not allow my mind to be occupied by the past, the future, or meaningless thinking in the present. Every mouthful of food nourishes me, my ancestors, and all my descendants who are present in me. As I chew I use this gatha:

Eating in the ultimate dimension
I am nourishing all my ancestors,
I am opening an upward path for all my descendants.

I nourish myself with edible food and with the food of sense impression. Edible food can bring me physical nourishment. Sense impression food can bring me joy and compassion as I am eating. When I eat in mindfulness I produce compassion, freedom, and joy, nourishing my Sangha and my family with these elements.

I shall not allow myself to eat or drink more than I need, as it is harmful for myself and for my practice. When I stand in line to take food or when I am putting food into my bowl, I vow to remember to practice taking only what I need and what will preserve peace and lightness in my body. As a monk or a nun, I know that my bowl is called the vessel of appropriate measure, and I practice only to take the amount of food that is enough.

Lord Buddha, when I look at the food I am eating I also see that the food is the gift of the earth and the sky. It is the result of hard work. As a monk or nun, I know it is the gift offered to me by laypeople and it is also the food the Buddha has given me to eat. When I became a monk or a nun you gave me a begging bowl, and you taught me that when I have this bowl I do not need to fear hunger if I practice sincerely. Lord Buddha, whenever I have finished eating, I hold my bowl and turn to you to offer words of thanks: "Thank you, Buddha, for giving me something to eat." When I say this, my heart is full of gratitude. Expressing gratitude to the Buddha is expressing gratitude to the earth, the sky, to all species, and to the hard work of many people, including my sister or brother who cooked this meal.

Touching the Earth

Lord Buddha, I touch the earth three times before you, the one who is worthy of all respect and offering, to express my gratitude to the earth, the sky, all species of living beings, and to nourish my happiness. [Bell]

26. Mindful Eating

Lord Buddha, when I am eating I remind myself that I should only eat what nourishes me and prevents illness. What I eat can make me healthy or make me sick. When I go shopping, when I cook, and when I eat, I shall give rise to mindfulness and not bring into my body the kind of food which makes me heavy and unwell. However appealing the food may be, if it is not healthy I shall not eat it. When I eat unhealthy food I put stress on my body and I make my ancestors and descendants in me feel heavy and oppressed.

Lord Buddha, while eating I shall also observe that I am eating with the aim of preserving my life. The aim of my life is to study and practice to transform my afflictions and to liberate people and all other species from their suffering. I shall receive food with this awareness. I shall remember with gratitude that I am receiving the food because I want to make progress on the path of love and understanding. Lord Buddha, when you sat and ate with the Sangha body you nourished happiness and compassion in yourself and in countless other beings. I value the time I have to eat together with the Sangha or with my family. I sit upright, at ease, and practice eating in such a way that I have joy, peace, and freedom as I eat. I eat slowly, aware of what I am eating, and I chew the food carefully, about thirty times, until it becomes liquid, and then I swallow it. From time to time I stop and look at my spiritual or blood family with whom I am eating. The powerful energy of mindfulness and concentration in the Sangha protects and supports me. While eating, I also produce the energy of mindfulness and concentration to nourish my Sangha body.

Lord Buddha, I know that you sat and ate in this way with your Sangha and I am sure that the monks and nuns were very happy sitting and eating in your presence, whether on the Vulture Peak, in the Bamboo Grove, in the Jeta Grove, or in the Great Forest near to the town of Vaishali. I know that today while I am sitting and eating with the Sangha, if I have enough mindfulness and concentration I shall also be able to see that I am eating with you, the Tathagata, and I shall be able to see you looking at me and smiling. Lord Buddha, I promise that I shall always eat together with the Sangha so my practice of mindfulness will be solid as I eat. I vow that I shall not eat alone in my room or at times when the Sangha is not eating except when I am sick or have some special service to perform which prevents me from returning home in time to eat with the Sangha.

Dear Buddha, I promise that I shall transform my habit of eating a snack whenever I feel some affliction such as loneliness or anxiety. I shall practice mindful breathing to recognize and embrace my feelings, rather than going to the refrigerator and taking food to fill up the vacuum in myself or to dissolve my anxiety.

Touching the Earth

Lord Buddha, I touch the earth three times before you to express my regret for how I have consumed in the past. I vow that I will eat and drink in the way that you have taught in order to be an example for my descendants. [Bell]

27. Mindfulness in Daily Life

Lord Buddha, at the time when you manifested on this Earth as Shakyamuni Buddha, you devoted your whole life to liberating beings from their suffering. At that time there were no airplanes, steamships, trains, or buses. In spite of this, you traveled on foot to visit the various small kingdoms in the plain of the Ganges. You walked wherever you wanted to go, taking every step in mindfulness. For the forty-five years during which you taught and practiced mindfulness, wherever you went you brought the energy of solidity and freedom. You liberated kings, ministers, generals, spiritual leaders, businessmen, intellectuals, rich and poor, as well as thieves, prostitutes, and butchers from their suffering. Your career of understanding and love has had a deep and lasting influence on so many generations of people throughout the world. I, your disciple, vow to practice sincerely with joy and peace so I can participate in the career of understanding and love which you have transmitted to me. I shall practice dwelling peacefully and happily in the present while I am sitting, walking, speaking, listening, eating, and working. I vow to practice mindfulness when I go to work, when I cook, do the laundry, sweep the courtyard, plant vegetables, drive the car, and do the shopping. I know that practicing mindfulness in all my daily activities brings lightness, joy, peace, and freedom into myself and everyone around me.

Lord Buddha, there are those of us who have to drive or take the train for one hour to get to work. At the end of the day it takes us another hour to get home. When we arrive, we are already tired. Then we still have to cook, eat, and clean up. Day after day we live like this; we are always busy. We also have to worry about paying the bills, the mortgage, the electricity, the water, the telephone, and taxes. There are also other problems like sickness, medicine, unemployment, and car accidents, which put a great deal of pressure on us in our daily lives, and cause us much anxiety and fear. Many of us are always in a hurry. We hurry to finish one thing to do something else, and one task always follows another. If we have nothing to do we cannot bear it so we fill our time with countless projects and errands. One hundred years flash past like a dream. I do not want to live like that. I want to live at ease and deeply every moment of my daily life. I want to practice living happily in the present moment. I want to do less work and to work in such a way so that every moment of my work brings me joy.

When I am driving I shall not allow myself to think about the past or the future, or allow my plans or anxieties to pull me away from reality. I shall follow my breathing and be aware that all my ancestors are in the car with me. For instance, I can imagine that my grandfather is driving with me, although in the past perhaps my grandfather did not know how to drive. I see my grandfather in me and I look at what is happening around me with the eyes of my grandfather. Lord Buddha, I also see that you are driving the car for me, and you drive very mindfully. Whenever I stop at a red light, I return to my breathing, relax, and smile. The red light is a bell of mindfulness, reminding me to return to the present moment. I feel gratitude to the red light as one of my practice friends reminding me to return to mindfulness. When there is a traffic jam I know how to breathe and smile, practicing: "I have arrived, I am home." Life is present in this moment. Every breath brings me back to the present moment to be in touch with life. I know that driving mindfully I shall not be tense, I shall have joy and the opportunity to look deeply. When other people are driving me I shall also practice like this. I shall follow my breathing, and I shall have an opportunity to be in touch with the wheat fields, the rolling hills, the rivers, or oceans that we are passing. I shall find skillful ways to remind the driver and other people who are in the car to practice with me so that throughout the journey we shall have the opportunity to produce mindfulness, concentration, and joy.

Touching the Earth

I touch the earth before Buddha Shikhin, Buddha Vishvabhu, and Buddha Krakkucchandha. [Bell]

28. Cooking with Mindfulness

Lord Buddha, whether I am cooking for the Sangha or for my family, I can practice mindfulness and the kitchen becomes my joyful meditation hall. When I put the water into the basin for washing the vegetables, I look deeply at the water to see its wonderful nature. I see that the water comes from high in the mountains or from deep within the earth right into our kitchen. I know that on this Earth there are places where there is a scarcity of water and people have to walk several miles just to carry back a pail of water on their shoulders. Here, water is available whenever I turn on the tap. If the water is cut off for a couple of hours, I already feel at a loss. Aware of the preciousness of clean water, I value the water that is available to me. I also value the electricity that I use to turn on a light or to boil water. I only need to be aware that there is water and electricity easily accessible to me, and I can be happy straightaway. When I am peeling vegetables or cooking them, I can do it in mindfulness and with love. I know that working with mindfulness and love, I shall know how to maintain my energy and not feel tired. When I see cooking as a way to offer nourishment and care to my family and friends, I will easily find joy and peace in the work. Looking deeply at the tomato, the carrot, or the piece of tofu, I can see the wonderful nature of these things, how they were nurtured by the soil, the sun, the rain, and the seed. As I make tea, I look deeply to see the hills of tea plants on the highlands in northern Vietnam or the misty hills in India. Working in silence with my friends and family together, we cook the meal with mindfulness, love, and joy. In the kitchen there is an altar to the kitchen bodhisattva, and whenever we begin to cook we can light a stick of incense to commence and continue the practice of cooking in the spiritual dimension.

World-Honored Buddha, I shall organize my life so that I shall have enough time and energy to cook in a leisurely and peaceful way. I promise that I shall not speak in the kitchen with irritation or in an unpleasant way. I am aware that the energy of love and harmony in the kitchen directly penetrates into the food that I am cooking and will offer to my beloved ones.

Touching the Earth

I touch the earth three times before the kitchen bodhisattva, asking the bodhisattva to bear witness to my vow to practice well in the kitchen. [Bell]

29. Right Livelihood

Lord Buddha, I wish to practice Right Livelihood. I vow that I shall not make my living in ways that destroy my compassion. As a practitioner of the first of the Five Mindfulness Trainings, I vow not to practice a profession that forces me to kill living beings or to destroy and pollute the environment. Neither shall I make my living in such a way that exploits and harms my fellow human beings. I vow that I shall not invest in companies that make profit for only a few people and deprive many others of their chance to live. I will not invest in companies that pollute the environment. I vow that I shall not make my living supported by the superstitions of others—selling charms and talismans, reading palms, telling fortunes, practicing as a medium, or exorcising spirits. As a monk or a nun, I shall not turn the practice of sending spiritual support to others into a way of making money. I shall not put a price on the services I perform at funerals or other ceremonies for the deceased. Lord Buddha, I promise that if I mistakenly fall into these ways of wrong livelihood or am forced by circumstances to make a living in these unwholesome ways, I shall find ways to disassociate myself from this wrong livelihood and begin a new profession that is in accord with the spirit of Right Livelihood. I know that if my career helps me nourish compassion every day and realize my ability to help others, then I shall be very happy as a teacher, nurse, doctor, environmentalist, research scientist, social worker, psychotherapist, or in any one of many other professions. Practicing Right Livelihood, I shall have an opportunity to practice understanding and love and to help free people and all beings from their suffering.

Lord Buddha, I vow to practice living simply, not consuming too much, so that I do not have to spend too much time making a living. I vow to give myself enough time to live deeply and freely while I am working. I vow not to immerse myself in many different occupations, taking on additional jobs to earn a little bit more money. I vow that I shall not look for happiness in being busy and consuming. I shall only look for happiness in the development of inner freedom and the practice of loving kindness. As a monk or a nun, I also need to be determined not to lose myself in the kind of work that I say is being done for the Buddha, but in fact is being done to seek praise, position, or benefit. Sometimes the work of building a temple, sculpting a statue, organizing the congregation, a ceremony, or a retreat can become a self-seeking activity. While I am doing work like this, I promise that I shall practice harmonizing my views and thoughts with those of other members of the Sangha. Building or organizational work is an opportunity for us to work together and practice letting go of our habit of thinking that only our own idea is good and the ideas of other people have no value.

I vow to listen deeply to the ideas of everyone in the community in order to arrive at a synthesis of ideas that forms a collective wisdom at the basis of every decision. If I do that, I shall be able to build more brotherhood and sisterhood and let go of self-pride and the feeling that I am a separate self. In this way I shall make progress on the path of transformation and healing. I know that when we can harmonize our various views and ideas, the work we do can be truly called work for the Buddha, the Dharma, and the Sangha. Work done in this spirit can liberate beings from their suffering and help others.

As a monk or a nun, I vow to not build a hermitage or temple where I would live apart from the rest of the Sangha, like a tiger who has left the forest. I shall only undertake work that has been entrusted to me by the Sangha and I vow that I shall work together in the spirit of peace and respect with my fellow practitioners in the Fourfold Sangha.

Lord Buddha, in the past I have made the mistake of losing myself in my work. I have worked to seek praise, power, and gain without even knowing what I was doing, always convincing myself that I was working for the Buddha. By paying close attention to your teachings I have woken up to my past errors and I sincerely express my regret.

Touching the Earth

Lord Buddha, with body, speech, and mind in perfect oneness, I touch the earth three times before you, the highest charioteer who has the capacity to master human beings, the Fully Awakened Teacher, the one whom the world honors. [Bell]

30. MINDFUL SEXUALITY

L ORD BUDDHA, in the past I did not know how to manage the
sexual energy in myself. This has caused me to make regret-
table mistakes. I know that the human species is an animal species
and that sexual energy is naturally present in all of us. In the past,
because I did not know the spiritual practice, I allowed the seeds of
sexuality in me to be watered too much. Sometimes sexual energy
arising in me has made me unstable. I may have read magazines or
books, or looked at films full of images that excite sexual energy. I
know that some people make themselves rich by selling sex, not only
in the form of selling bodies, but in the form of selling sounds and
images.

Images that call up sexual desire are everywhere, in books, magazines, television, movies, advertisements, DVDs, and on the Internet.
Young people, particularly, are the victims of this kind of marketing.
The seeds of sexual energy in them are watered many times every day.
The number of young men and women, often from age thirteen or
younger, who are pulled into the net of unhealthy sexual activity is
alarming. It is a true catastrophe when young people know sex but do
not know how to love. When young people who have practiced empty
sex grow up they never have a chance to know the joy of true love. The
habit of masturbation leads to similar results. It dries up the source of

wholesome energy of body and mind and does not give a person the chance to know what true love is.*

Lord Buddha, you have taught us the truth that body and mind are one reality, and I know that whatever happens to my body also happens to my mind. I vow to look after my body and mind and not allow the seeds of sexual desire to be watered in myself, and not to fall into the habit of masturbation. I vow that from now on I shall not read books or magazines or look at films that excite sexual energy. I shall not listen to or tell stories with sexual overtones. I shall not use the telephone or the computer to find sounds and images that arouse sexual desire. I also vow to lend my energy to action that makes people aware of the harm done by the artificial arousal of sexual energy. I vow to do everything that I can to create a healthy environment at all levels of society, especially for the younger generation. Lord Buddha, I ask you to guide me with the light of understanding and compassion in this work.

Touching the Earth

With body, speech, and mind in perfect oneness, I touch the earth before the elders Upali, Purna, and Mahagotami. [Bell]

---

* In the Buddhist tradition, monks and nuns are celibate and within the monastic code masturbation is prohibited. Although masturbation may not be unwholesome in and of itself for laypeople, as an excessive practice it can drain one's energy, which may otherwise be used for developing one's *bodhicitta*, the heart and mind of love and compassionate action. We can all be aware of sexual energy when it arises and redirect it by staying present and focusing on the breath.

31. Healing Old Sexual Energy

Lord Buddha, obscured by ignorance during this lifetime and lifetimes before, as a society we have not been able to see that the energy of sexual desire, if it is not recognized and properly managed, will destroy the family, the society, and the body and mind of the individual. In our ignorance we have not been able to protect our bodies and minds from unhealthy sex, because we have not created a wholesome cultural and social environment. Without intention, we have acted in opposition to the Third Mindfulness Training concerning sexual misconduct. We have sexually abused children, including our own children.* We have brought about division and suffering which has lasted from one generation to another.

Today, I have woken up to my mistakes and express my deep regret. I vow to learn and to practice the Dharma doors the Lord Buddha has shown us, to master my body and mind, and to make my environment a healthy one. I shall practice to use the energy of my body and mind to develop my understanding and compassion. With understanding and compassion, I shall liberate beings from their suffering and help the world. I know that if bodhicitta, the mind of love, is in me, and my

---

* In the Third Mindfulness Training, we make the determination not to commit sexual misconduct and also to do everything in our power to prevent children from being sexually abused and to keep couples and families from being broken by sexual misconduct. Ending the great suffering due to sexual misconduct is not only a matter of our personal behavior, but of a collective awakening. This meditation is written in this spirit.

deep aspiration to liberate beings from their suffering is strong, nearly all of my energy will go in that direction. When the energy of compassion is strong in me, the sexual energy in me will not have the strength to bring about destruction for myself and for people around me.

Touching the Earth

Lord Buddha, with body, speech, and mind in perfect oneness, I touch the earth three times before you and the holy Sangha throughout all generations. [Bell]

32. Transforming Sexual Misconduct

Lord Buddha, may you and the bodhisattvas open up your heart of love towards me and support me spiritually. Give me the strength to help society through this dark time of much sexual misconduct. I am aware that if I do not have a strong practice of mindfulness when my senses are receiving sensual impressions, sexual desire will be aroused in me every day. Whenever that energy is aroused, my body and mind are no longer protected because the sexual energy will push me to find ways of satisfying it.

Sexual misconduct is destroying millions of lives every year and if I do not practice mindfulness, I can easily become a victim of it. Our world is being burned by the fire of sexual misconduct. I am aware that illnesses such as HIV/AIDS and other sexually transmitted diseases have created enormous suffering all over the world. I vow to do everything in my power to contribute to lessening the suffering of such illnesses and to prevent HIV/AIDS and other sexually transmitted diseases from being transmitted in the future. I bow my head and ask the Buddha and the bodhisattva Avalokiteshvara to, out of compassion, rain down on our planet drops of the nectar of great love. I know that only when there is true love, responsibility, and awareness can we save our world from this situation.

Touching the Earth

With body, speech, and mind in perfect oneness, I touch the earth three times before the Bodhisattva of Great Compassion, Avalokiteshvara. May the energy of great compassion transform and put an end to the obstacles brought about by sexual misconduct. [Bell]

33. Sexual Responsibility

Lord Buddha, as monks and nuns we are fortunate to be able to practice living a life of chastity. The precepts and the fine manners protect us and do not allow us to be sucked down into the bog of sexual misconduct.* As laypeople, we aren't able to live twenty-four hours a day in an environment where everyone is practicing mindfulness. That is why we have to practice the Third Mindfulness Training with great determination, so that we do not allow our thinking or the images and sounds around us to water the seeds of sexual misconduct in us.

Dear Buddha, I vow to use my free time to learn about your teachings. I shall participate in Dharma discussions and organize practice sessions for the Sangha, or take part in cultural and social activities whose function is to help the world and to help us relieve our suffering. Whenever I have an opportunity I shall go to a monastery or practice center to participate in retreats, listen to Dharma talks, and take part in Dharma discussions. I vow that I shall always be present for recitations of the Mindfulness Trainings. I vow to nourish the mind of love in me so that it grows greater every day. I know that when the energy of understanding and love in me is powerful I shall not fall under the influence of the forces of sexual misconduct in me.

* For a full list and explanation of the mindful manners for novice monks and nuns, see Thich Nhat Hanh, *Stepping into Freedom* (Berkeley, CA: Parallax Press, 1998).

Lord Buddha, as monks and nuns, we know clearly that the ideal of a monk or a nun can only be realized when we wholly put aside all the ties of worldly love. I vow to practice all the mindfulness trainings and the fine manners I have received to protect myself and others. I know that sexual activity will destroy my life as a monk or a nun, will harm the lives of others, and will not allow me to realize my ideal of helping beings be free from their suffering. I vow that I shall never dismiss the practice of the fine manners, thinking that I have enough inner freedom and spiritual strength not to need their protection. I know that attachment will lead to sexual desire. The forms of attachment can be very subtle. If I do not protect myself with the practice of fine manners, then I may develop attachments that will cause the quality of my practice and that of the whole Sangha to go down. I am aware that an attachment can cause me to lose my peace in body and mind and will rob me of the opportunity to love all beings with equanimity and compassion. When I am attached I lose my freedom and I cause the other person to lose his or her freedom. As a monk or a nun, I vow not to allow myself to be alone with someone of the opposite sex. When I feel some emotional attachment towards someone, I shall not seek opportunities to be close to them and say or do things that will water the seeds of attachment in myself and in the other person, whether that person is a monk, nun, or layperson.

I know that as fellow disciples of the Buddha, we have to look at each other as brothers and sisters of one family. Brotherhood and sisterhood can nourish us and protect us on the path of practice and help us to offer the teachings of love and understanding to the world. Lord Buddha, I promise that as far as emotional attachment is concerned, I shall never go further than brotherhood and sisterhood. I shall see the precepts, the fine manners, and the support and guidance of fellow practitioners in the Fourfold Sangha as my only true protection, helping me to build brotherhood and sisterhood and preventing me from falling into wrong attachment. I vow that I shall always listen carefully to guidance that I receive from my teacher and my Sangha to help me wake up. Whenever a member of the Sangha reminds me that I am showing signs of being emotionally attached, I shall join my palms and receive this reminder gratefully. I shall not try to find a way to excuse myself, or blame or be angry with the person who has reminded me.

Touching the Earth

Lord Buddha, with body, speech, and mind in perfect oneness, I touch the earth three times before you and before the Vinaya Master Upali. [Bell]

34. Faith and Right Energy

Lord Buddha, I have great faith in you, in your teachings, and in the community of practice. Whenever I use your teachings and apply them in my daily life I see how my afflictions are calmed and transformed. I see how the energy of mindfulness, concentration, and insight in me is always growing, helping me to overcome my difficulties and sorrow. My faith is built upon my living experience and not on something promised for the future. My faith is an energy based on clear understanding and not on superstition. When I practice and I experience peace, joy, and healing, my faith grows stronger, bringing me great happiness. You have taught that a mule or a camel forced to carry heavy burdens does not suffer as much as someone who, out of ignorance, does not know his direction in life. Not to have a direction in life is the greatest suffering. I do have faith in my path of practice; I do have a direction to go in. I do not need to live in confusion and fear, and this is the greatest happiness I could hope for. There are many people in the world who are suffering. They are destroying their own bodies and minds because they do not have faith and they do not have a path to go on.

Lord Buddha, I want my practice of mindfulness and my actions of body, speech, and mind to enable me every day to advance courageously on the path of transformation and healing for myself and for the world. I know that the energy of faith can help me to do this.

I vow to practice Right Energy. I vow not to water the negative seeds of infatuation, violence, and hatred in me by being in touch with and consuming toxic items. I do not want to give the seeds of infatuation, hatred, and violence an opportunity to be watered, to develop and grow strong. I want to practice right attention and only give my attention to thoughts, energies, and sounds that can water the wholesome seeds in me.

If by chance the negative seeds in me are watered and develop into mental formations, I shall do my best to find a way for those mental formations to return to the depths of my consciousness in the form of seeds. I know that if these mental formations arise frequently, they will quickly grow strong, while if they are allowed to lie still for a long time in the depths of my consciousness they will grow weaker. You have taught us to practice right attention, to bring bright and beautiful mental formations back again into our conscious mind, and to allow them to replace the unwholesome mental formations. By my study and recitation of the sutras, and by being close to noble practitioners, I shall help the bright and beautiful mental formations to arise frequently and I shall find ways to help these mental formations to remain as long as possible in my mind consciousness. I know that if the positive mental formations of loving kindness, compassion, joy, and equanimity are developed and maintained, they will have an opportunity to grow. Their growth will give rise to transformation that will bring me and those around me much happiness.

World-Honored Buddha, you have taught me how I can produce the five kinds of spiritual energy: faith, diligence, mindfulness, concentration, and insight. The energy of faith leads to the energy of diligence. When there is diligence, the energies of mindfulness, concentration, and insight will be produced and will increase the energy of faith. I touch the earth before the Lord Buddha and the holy Sangha as I make the vow that I shall practice every day to produce and strengthen these precious energies inside me.

Touching the Earth

Homage to our root teacher, Buddha Shakyamuni. [Bell]

Homage to the teacher of Great Understanding, Shariputra. [Bell]

Homage to the teacher of Great Eloquence, Purna. [Bell]

35. How to Study

Lord Buddha, we all like to study. But why do we study? Often it is because we are looking for some advantage such as attaining a privileged position in society rather than to open our mind and discover methods of practice that can help us transform our own suffering and that of society. Some people devote themselves to their studies because they want a diploma or they want to win debates and prove that they are someone who has studied widely. I may have met people who speak very fluently about the deep teachings in the sutras and the different schools of thought in Buddhism. They can give eloquent teachings on no-self, impermanence, compassion, loving kindness, and liberation, but they continue to be prejudiced, angry, proud, and jealous. They do not know how to listen deeply and use loving speech. They are not able to transform the afflictions in their own mind and they make other people suffer.

Lord Buddha, I do not want to be that kind of student. The reason I want to listen to and learn the teachings of the Buddha is to realize liberation in myself, transform my afflictions, and produce understanding and love. Lord Buddha, in the Sutra on Knowing the Better Way to Catch a Snake you have taught that I should not study spiritual teachings with the aim of winning debates.* We should study with

---

* For sutra and commentary, see Thich Nhat Hanh, *Thundering Silence* (Berkeley, CA: Parallax Press, 1993).

the aim of transforming our suffering and liberating ourselves. I vow that whenever I study the sutras, especially the Mahayana sutras and commentaries, I shall always ask myself the question: "Do these deep and mystical teachings have anything to do with the suffering which is in me and which I experience in my everyday life? How can I study this sutra so that I can bring it into my daily life and use the words to transform my afflictions and resolve my present difficulties?"

Touching the Earth

I touch the earth three times before the elders Subhuti, Ananda, and Rahula. [Bell]

36. STUDYING WITH PURPOSE

LORD BUDDHA, my insight and understanding concerning the Three Jewels—Buddha, Dharma, and Sangha—is still very shallow. I can only understand fully what it means to take refuge in the Three Jewels when I have looked deeply. As my insight and understanding of the Three Jewels grows deeper every day, my practice of taking refuge will increasingly bring about more solidity, peace, and happiness. Taking refuge in the Buddha, Dharma, and Sangha is not just a belief or a ceremony, but is a daily practice. Every moment of my daily life can be a moment to practice taking refuge in the Three Jewels. Placing myself under the protection of the Three Jewels, I feel safeguarded, solid, happy, and free.

When the energy of the Three Jewels is present in me, the practice of the Mindfulness Trainings and the fine manners do not present any hardship. Lord Buddha, you have taught in the Sutra on the White-Clad Disciple that the practice of the Three Refuges and the Five Mindfulness Trainings can bring happiness in the present moment.* I have solid faith that this is true because I have experienced it for myself. I vow to practice the refuges and the trainings deeply and to help my loved ones to do the same. You gave many teachings to your lay disciples and I shall devote time to studying these sutras. I shall

---

* For sutra and commentary, see Thich Nhat Hanh, *For a Future to Be Possible* (Berkeley, CA: Parallax Press, 2007).

also study the sutras that you taught the monks and nuns in order to gain a deep understanding of the Four Noble Truths, the Noble Eight-fold Path, the Five Faculties, the Five Powers, the Seven Elements of Enlightenment, the Six Paramitas, and the Middle Way of Interde-pendent Arising. Lord Buddha, you have said that laypeople can also practice in order to be liberated from birth and death and arrive at the understanding of the unborn and the undying, if they know how to organize their daily life to leave enough time for the practice. I vow that in Dharma discussion, I shall make an effort to listen deeply to the experience of others, and when I share, I shall not try to flaunt my knowledge or be caught up in debating and disputing, but only present my own experience of the practice in the light of the teach-ings I have received.

Lord Buddha, as a monk or a nun I vow to learn and practice to become a true teacher of the Way, able to liberate others from their suffering and help the world. Many people have finished a doctorate in higher Buddhist studies, but their knowledge about Buddhism has not helped them to transform their afflictions and produce peace and happiness. I vow to give priority to studying those subjects that I can apply in my daily practice, and that whatever I study in addition will also be able to guide me on the path. I do not want to study only to become a scholar of wide knowledge. Lord Buddha, I shall study with the purpose of transforming my afflictions and to have enough expe-rience so that I can help others transform their afflictions. I know that in this way I can continue the Buddha's career.

Lord Buddha, in the past I have gone astray in the way I have stud-ied. Now I make the aspiration to turn back to the path that you have shown me.

Touching the Earth

Lord Buddha, I touch the earth before you, the one who understands the world deeply, before Manjushri Bodhisattva, and the Venerable Ananda. [Bell]

37. Living in the Buddha's House

Lord Buddha, I know that because of the merit of my ancestors, in this lifetime I have had the good fortune to be your disciple and participate in your work of understanding and loving. My spiritual family is extensive. It includes the bodhisattvas, the holy Sangha, and countless generations of both monastic and lay disciples. Having been born into your family, I am able to abide in the house of the Tathagata, wear the clothes of the Tathagata, eat the food of the Tathagata, and do the work of the Tathagata. I vow to live in such a way that at every moment of my daily life this awareness is fully present. Whenever I sit in mindfulness with my back upright, my body and mind at ease, and a smile of awakening on my lips, I am sitting in the house of the Tathagata. It is not necessary to sit in the meditation hall to sit in the Tathagata's house; I can be in the classroom, in the park, in the train station, in a meeting, using the computer, or driving a car. If I know how to sit mindfully, wherever I sit I am in your house. Whenever I return to my breathing, produce mindfulness and concentration, and am able to be nourished by the energy of peace and joy, I am in the house of the Tathagata. Wherever I walk with solid, free, peaceful, and joyful footsteps, I am walking in the house of the Tathagata. When I am cooking, washing clothes, or tidying up, I need not leave the house of the Tathagata. Whether I am a layperson or a monk or a nun, I have the right to live twenty-four hours a day in the house of the Tathagata.

The clothing I wear does not have to be a ceremonial robe to be called the clothing of the Tathagata. When I wear the clothes of mindfulness, the clothes of the mindfulness trainings, the clothes of modesty, the clothes of a simple and humble life, I am wearing the clothes of the Tathagata. No other kind of clothing is as beautiful and as warm as this. Whenever I eat a meal, giving rise to the mind of gratitude, I am able to nourish the Tathagata in myself and nourish my teacher and my Sangha. When I eat like this I am eating the food of the Tathagata. As I am eating the food of the Tathagata, I nourish my body and mind and the body and mind of all generations who have gone before me as well as all generations to come.

As a monk or a nun, I know that from the time I receive the three robes and bowl I shall never need to be afraid of being hungry or cold or not having a house to live in, because I have been accepted in the house of the Tathagata. I have the clothes of the Tathagata to wear and the food of the Tathagata to eat. I know that if I receive and observe the mindfulness trainings and the fine manners, the Fourfold Sangha will nourish me, give me food to eat and clothes to wear.

Lord Buddha, I know that for as long as I feel gratitude, I am happy. I am very grateful to have been introduced to the Three Jewels. The Buddha, Dharma, and Sangha have rescued, nourished, and protected me. I feel gratitude to my parents, teachers, friends, and all living beings. I feel grateful to everyone who has given me the environment and the conditions in which I can practice, transform, and help people to be liberated from their suffering. I vow to live diligently with enough awakening to be able to remember how fortunate I am and how many favorable causes and conditions I have to practice and to be happy. I vow to practice awareness so that the flame of gratitude is always in my heart and I never become ungrateful, full of discontent and criticism. Mindfulness helps me to feel gratitude and because of this I can live happily every moment of my daily life.

Touching the Earth

Lord Buddha, I ask you, the one who has understood the world deeply, the holy Sangha, and my ancestors, to be my witness as I touch the earth three times. [Bell]

38. PROTECTING THE EARTH

L ORD BUDDHA, you are a child of the Earth and you have chosen it to be the place of your enlightenment and of teaching the practice. In the process of practicing and teaching, you have trained countless bodhisattvas who have the capacity to protect this planet and keep it beautiful. I remember how, in the presence of the Lotus Sutra assembly, you summoned all the bodhisattvas, and hundreds of thousands of them sprang up from the depths of the Earth. These bodhisattvas promised you that they would remain and look after this planet forever and would also continue your career of understanding and love.

Lord Buddha, I am also a child of the Earth, and I also want to contribute to protecting our beautiful planet. I want in some way to be one of the countless bodhisattvas who spring up from the Earth. I vow to remain with the Sangha in this world to do the work of liberating living beings from suffering. I ask in this moment that the mountains and rivers be my witness as I bow my head and ask the Lord of Compassion to accept and embrace me. I have manifested from the Earth and I shall return to Mother Earth and continue to manifest millions of times again, so that, together with the Sangha body, I can do the work of transforming garbage into flowers, protecting life, and building a Pure Land right here on Earth. I know that understanding and love are the basic things needed for building the Pure Land. Therefore I vow that in every moment of my daily life, I will make an effort to produce the energy of understanding and love.

Touching the Earth

Lord Buddha, I shall touch the earth three times to solidify my commitment to Mother Earth. [Bell]

39. Oneness with the Earth

Lord Buddha, looking deeply at the Earth I see the light and warmth of the sun that allows everything to be born and grow. I also see the streams of fresh water that flow on this planet and bring life to the Earth. I also sense the presence of the atmosphere and all the elements in space, like oxygen, carbon dioxide, hydrogen, and nitrogen. Without the atmosphere, the water, and the sun there could not be the beautiful adornments of the Earth, the green willow, the purple bamboo, and the yellow flowers. I see everywhere the four elements of earth, water, fire, and air, how they interrelate with everything and inter-are in me. I shall touch the earth and remain close to the earth to see that I am one with Mother Earth; I am one with the sunlight, the rivers, the lakes, the ocean, and the clouds in the sky. The four elements in my body and the four elements in the body of the cosmos are not separate. I vow to return and take refuge in Mother Earth to see her solid and resilient nature within myself.

Touching the Earth

I touch the earth before the bodhisattva Dharanimdhara, Earth Holder, and the bodhisattva Kshitigarbha, Earth Store. [Bell]

40. RESCUING ALL BEINGS

Lord Buddha, as your disciple, I have the bodhisattva Kshitigarbha as an elder brother. Kshitigarbha is a great bodhisattva who made a deep vow: He would not stop the work of rescuing beings from the hell realms until they were empty. Lord Buddha, Kshitigarbha is a good name for this bodhisattva. It means Earth Store and implies a store of the qualities of stability, expansiveness, and the capacity to contain and embrace all things. Just as suffering and afflictions have no limit, the bodhisattva's deep aspiration and action to rescue beings from this suffering also has no limit. For as long as there is suffering, there are afflictions that cause suffering. The bodhisattvas do not cease rescuing beings from their suffering. Our own planet Earth needs people like the bodhisattva Kshitigarbha, and I myself want to help this bodhisattva. I see that the hell realms of misunderstanding, hatred, and violence exist everywhere. And yet, everywhere I can find bodhisattvas who are striving to dismantle them.

Lord Buddha, there was a time when you taught the Venerable Rahula to learn to act as the earth. You said: "Rahula, you should learn how to be like the earth. When people pour or sprinkle on the earth fragrant and pure substances like perfume and fragrant milk, the earth does not feel proud. And when people pour upon the earth unclean and bad-smelling substances like excrement, urine, blood, pus, or phlegm the earth does not feel anger, hatred, or shame. The earth has the capacity to receive, embrace, and transform everything."

The bodhisattva Kshitigarbha also has the energy of solidity and inclusiveness like the earth, and therefore the bodhisattva is able to embrace and transform everything. I also want to learn to be like the earth, as the bodhisattva Kshitigarbha and the Venerable Rahula have done. We all have painful feelings of shame, sadness, and apathy. I touch the earth so that the earth can embrace me along with all my shame, sadness, weariness, and pain. With the help of the earth, I vow gradually to transform this shame, apathy, and pain, so that in time to come the fruits of love and joy may appear on this Earth and in my own heart.

Touching the Earth

Homage to the bodhisattva Kshitigarbha, who with great solidity and strength embraces all those who suffer, and to Rahula, who humbly hid his deep understanding. [Bell]

41. The Earth as a Solid Place of Refuge

World-Honored Buddha, just before you realized the path at the foot of the bodhi tree, Mara appeared and asked you questions with the aim of making you abandon your aspiration.

Mara asked: "Who are you to dare to think that you will realize the fruit of the highest awakening? Even someone who has practiced for countless lifetimes would not dare to think that in twenty-four hours they would be able to realize the fruits of the path. Who can be witness to the fact that what you say is the truth?"

Lord Buddha, when Mara asked you these questions, you put your right hand down and touched the earth and you said to Mara: "The earth is my witness that what I say is the truth." At that moment the earth shook and Mara retreated. Lord Buddha, the image of you sitting solidly on the earth with your right hand in the position of Touching the Earth brings up so much respect in me.* Every time I see this image of you I feel moved. The Earth has witnessed your appearance on this planet for countless lifetimes and your practice of the spiritual path has been successful in every lifetime.

Lord Buddha, the Earth has been a solid place of refuge for you to manifest millions of times in your wonderful transformation bodies. In the past you were Buddha Vipashyin, just as in the future you

---

* This position of the hand, loose and draped over the knee to touch the ground, is known as the *bhumisparsha mudra*, the seal of Touching the Earth.

will be Buddha Maitreya. In every lifetime you have manifested from the earth and taken refuge in the earth. I also can take refuge in the earth and in doing so I will also have your energy of solidity and great acceptance.

Praising the Buddha

The Buddha Jewel shines infinitely.
He has realized enlightenment for countless lifetimes.
The beauty and stability of a Buddha sitting can be seen in
   mountains and rivers.
How splendid is the Vulture Peak!

How beautiful the light that shines forth from Buddha's third eye,
illuminating the six dark paths.
The Nagapushpa Assembly will be our next appointment
for the continuation of the true teachings and practices.
We take refuge in the Buddha ever-present.

Lord Buddha, I know that practicing touching the earth as I sit, walk, or lie down, I can realize your energy and I can continue the career of the Tathagata.

Touching the Earth

Lord Buddha, allow me to touch the earth three times to be in touch with the earth deeply and to feel its energy of unlimited solidity and inclusiveness. [Bell]

42. Encouragement on the Path

Lord Buddha, I have heard your encouraging words. I will practice sitting solidly on this earth and practice touching the earth deeply and calmly.

*Earth Touching**

Here is the foot of a tree.
Here is an empty, quiet place.
Here is a small sitting cushion.
Here is the cool green of the grass.
My child, why don't you sit down?

Sit upright.
Sit with solidity.
Sit in peace.
Don't let your thoughts lift you up into the air.
Sit so that you can really touch the Earth
and be one with her.
You may like to smile, my child.

---

* "Earth Touching" by Thich Nhat Hanh can be found in *Call Me by My True Names* (Berkeley, CA: Parallax Press, 1999), pp. 197–199.

Earth will transmit to you her solidity,
her peace, and her joy.
With your mindful breathing,
with your peaceful smile,
you sustain the mudra of Earth Touching.

There were times when you didn't do well.
Sitting on earth, it was as if you were floating in the air,
you who used to wander in the cycle of birth and death,
drifting and sinking in the ocean of misperceptions.
But Earth is always patient
and one-hearted.
Earth is still waiting for you
because Earth has been waiting for you
during the last trillion lives.
That is why she can wait for you for any length of time.
She will always welcome you,
always fresh and green, exactly like the first time,
because love never says, "This is the last";
because Earth is a loving mother.
She will never stop waiting for you.

Do go back to her, my child.
You will be like that tree.
The leaves, the branches, and the flowers of your soul
will be fresh and green
once you enter the mudra of Earth Touching.

The empty path welcomes you, my child,
filled with grass and little flowers,
the path among the fragrant rice paddy
that you walked on, holding your mother's hand,
is still impressed in your mind.
Walk leisurely, peacefully.
Your feet should deeply touch the earth.
Don't let your thoughts lift you up into the air, my child.
Go back to the path every moment.
The path is your dearest friend.
She will transmit to you
her strength,
her peace.

Your diligent awareness of your breathing
will keep you in touch with the earth.
Walk as if you were kissing the earth with your feet,
as if you were massaging the earth.
The marks left by your feet
will be like the emperor's seal
calling the Now to come back to the Here;
so that life will be present,
so that the blood will bring the color of love to your face,
so that the wonders of life will be manifested,
and all afflictions will be transformed into
peace and joy.

There were times when you did not succeed, my child.
Walking on the empty path, you were floating in the air,
because you used to get lost in samsara
and drawn into the world of illusion.
But the beautiful path is always patient.
It is always waiting for you to come back,
the path which is familiar to you,
the path which is so faithful.
It knows deeply that you will come back one day.
It will be joyful to welcome you back.
It will be as fresh and as beautiful as the first time.
Love never says, "This is the last."

That path is you, my child.
That is why it will never be tired of waiting.
Whether it is covered now with red dust
or with autumn leaves
or icy snow—
do go back to the path, my child,
because I know
you will be like that tree,
the leaves, the trunk, the branches,
and the blossoms of your soul
will be fresh and beautiful,
once you enter the mudra of Earth Touching.

I vow that from now on I shall see the earth as my solid foundation
whenever I practice touching the earth, sitting, or walking meditation.

Touching the Earth

Lord Buddha, I shall touch and stay close to the earth. I shall entrust myself wholly to the earth. [Bell]

43. THE RIVER OF LIFE

LORD BUDDHA, I am aware that in me there is a river of life that contains my ancestors and my descendants. All generations of my spiritual and blood ancestors are present in me. I am their continuation. I do not have a separate self. I am practicing to let go of everything that I think is myself or belongs to me, so that I can become one with this river of life. This river of life is flowing in me. My spiritual ancestors are the Buddha, the bodhisattvas, the holy community of practice and ancestral teachers throughout all generations. That river includes my spiritual teachers of this lifetime, whether they are still on this Earth or whether they have passed away. They are present in me. They have transmitted to me seeds of peace, understanding, love, and happiness. Thanks to them I have the resource of peace, joy, insight, and compassion within me, even if it is still small. In the river of my spiritual ancestors, there are those whose practice of the precepts, understanding, and compassion is fully realized. There are also those whose practice of precepts, understanding, and compassion has had shortcomings. I bow my head and accept all my spiritual ancestors, realized and not realized, because in myself there are weaknesses and shortcomings as far as the practice of precepts, understanding, and compassion is concerned. I open my heart and accept all my spiritual descendants, those whose practice of precepts and understanding is worthy of praise as well as those who are difficult for me and have ups and downs on their path of practice.

I accept all my ancestors on my mother's and my father's sides of the family with all their virtues, meritorious actions, and shortcomings. I also open my heart and accept all my blood descendants with their virtues, their talents, and their shortcomings. My spiritual and blood descendants and my spiritual and blood ancestors are all present in me. I am they and they are me. I do not have a separate self. We are all present in a wonderful stream of life that is constantly flowing and changing in a marvelous way.

Touching the Earth

Lord Buddha, I touch the earth three times to let go of the idea that I am a self separate from my ancestors and my descendants, and to release all the irritation and anger that I still hold towards them. [Bell]

44. Oneness with All Beings

Lord Buddha, I see that I am part of the wonderful pattern of life that stretches out in all directions. I see my close relationship with every person and every species. The happiness and suffering of all humans and all other species are my own happiness and suffering. I am one with someone who has been born disabled, or someone who is disabled because of war, accident, or sickness. I am one with people who are caught in situations of war, oppression, and exploitation. I am one with people who have never found happiness in their family and society. They do not have roots; they do not have peace of mind; they are hungry for understanding and love. They are looking for something beautiful, true, and wholesome to hold on to and to believe in. I am one with people at their last breath who are afraid because they do not know where they are going. I am the child living in miserable poverty and disease, whose legs and arms are as thin as sticks, without any future. I am also the person who is producing armaments to sell to poor countries.

I am the frog swimming in the lake, but I am also the water snake who needs to nourish its body with the body of the frog. I am the caterpillar and the ant, but I am also the bird who is looking for the caterpillar and the ant to eat. I am the forest that is being cut down, the water and the air that are being polluted. I am also the one who cuts down the forest and pollutes the water and the air. I see myself in all species and all species in myself.

I am one with the great beings who have witnessed the truth of no birth and no death, who are able to look at the appearances of birth, death, happiness, and suffering with calm eyes. I am one with the wise and good people who are present a little bit everywhere in this world. I am one with those who are in touch with what is wonderful and can nourish and heal life. I am one with those who are able to embrace the whole of this world with their heart of love and their two arms of caring action. I am a person who has enough peace, joy, and freedom to be able to offer fearlessness and the joy of life to living beings around me. I see that I am not alone. The love and the joy of great beings present in this world are supporting me and not allowing me to drown in despair. They help me to live my life peacefully and joyfully, fully and meaningfully. I see myself in all the great beings and all the great beings in myself.

Touching the Earth

Lord Buddha, I shall touch the earth three times to recognize that I am one with all the great bodhisattvas who are presently on this Earth and to receive their tremendous energy. I also touch the earth to be in touch with the suffering of all species so that the energy of compassion can arise and grow in me. [Bell]

45. Limitless Life

Lord Buddha, I see that this body made of the four elements is not really me and I am not limited by this body. I am the whole of the river of life of blood and spiritual ancestors that has been continuously flowing for thousands of years and flows on for thousands of years into the future. I am one with my ancestors and my descendants. I am life that is manifest in countless different forms. I am one with all species whether they are peaceful and joyful or suffering and afraid. I am present everywhere in this world. I have been present in the past and will be there in the future. The disintegration of this body does not touch me, just as when the petals of the plum blossom fall it does not mean the end of the plum tree. I see that I am like a wave on the surface of the ocean. I see myself in all the other waves, and all the other waves in myself. The manifestation or the disappearance of the wave does not lessen the presence of the ocean. My Dharma body and spiritual life are unborn and undying. I am able to see the presence of myself before this body manifested and after this body has disintegrated. I am able to see the presence of myself outside of this body, even in the present moment. Eighty or ninety years is not my lifetime. My lifetime, like that of a leaf or of a Buddha, is immeasurable. I am able to go beyond the idea that I am a body separate from all other manifestations of life, in time and in space.

Touching the Earth

Lord Buddha, I touch the earth three times to see the no birth, no death nature of myself and let go of the idea that I am a body separate from all other manifestations of life. [Bell]

46. Riding the Waves of Birth and Death

Lord Buddha, as I talk to you I think of you manifesting as Shakyamuni Buddha 2,600 years ago. I know that you are still there in hundreds of thousands of different transformation bodies. I also know that you are present in me and I am your continuation. I am one of the countless transformation bodies of the Buddha. Thanks to you opening my eyes, I know that you are not limited by time and space and your life span is limitless. The changing appearances of birth and death do not touch the Tathagata because the Tathagata has realized the unborn. I know that if I continue to be in touch with my own nature of no birth and no death I shall also see that my life span is immeasurable. I also can ride freely on the waves of birth and death like the great bodhisattvas. When I have realized the unborn and the undying, then the changing appearances of birth and death will no longer be able to touch me. I promise you that I shall practice diligently. I shall not get caught up in worldly matters and plans that take away my time and opportunity to practice. I ask you to be my witness and support me. I touch the earth to express my deep gratitude to the Buddha for listening to me and supporting me during my practice.

Touching the Earth

I touch the earth three times to recognize the limitless life span of the Tathagata, the one who has come from suchness, and to recognize that my own life span is also limitless. [Bell]

Three Touching the Earth Ceremonies for Beginning Anew*

* Audio recordings of most of the ceremonial chants in this book can be found on the CD
Chanting Breath by Breath (Berkeley, CA: Parallax Press, 2002).

CEREMONY 1

{Incense Offering (Version Two), Touching the Earth, Sutra Opening Verse, The Heart of Perfect Understanding, Guided Meditations 1–17, Protecting and Transforming, Gatha for Beginning Anew, Taking Refuge, Sharing the Merit}

Opening the Ceremony

INCENSE OFFERING (Version Two)

The fragrance of this incense
invites the awakened mind
to be truly present with us now.
The fragrance of this incense
fills our practice center,
protects and guards our mind
from all wrong thinking.
The fragrance of this incense
collects us and unites us.
Precepts, concentration, and insight
we offer for all that is
Namo Bodhisattvebhyah
Namo Mahasattvebhyah

TOUCHING THE EARTH

Opening Gatha

The one who bows and the one who is bowed to
are both, by nature, empty.
Therefore the communication between them
is inexpressibly perfect.
Our practice center is the Net of Indra
reflecting all Buddhas everywhere.
And with my person in front of each Buddha,
I go with my whole life for refuge. [Bell]

Prostrations

Offering light in the Ten Directions,
the Buddha, the Dharma, and the Sangha,
to whom we bow in gratitude. [Bell]

Teaching and living the way of awareness
in the very midst of suffering and confusion,
Shakyamuni Buddha, the Fully Enlightened One,
to whom we bow in gratitude. [Bell]

Cutting through ignorance, awakening our hearts
    and our minds,
Manjushri, the Bodhisattva of Great Understanding,
to whom we bow in gratitude. [Bell]

Working mindfully, working joyfully for the sake of all beings,
Samantabhadra, the Bodhisattva of Great Action,
to whom we bow in gratitude. [Bell]

Listening deeply, serving beings in countless ways,
Avalokiteshvara, the Bodhisattva of Great Compassion,
to whom we bow in gratitude. [Bell]

Fearless and persevering through realms of suffering and darkness,
Kshitigarbha, the Bodhisattva of Great Aspiration,
to whom we bow in gratitude. [Bell]

Seed of awakening and loving kindness in children and all beings,
Maitreya, the Buddha to-be-born,
To whom we bow in gratitude. [Bell]

Convener of the Sangha, the teacher Mahakashyapa,
to whom we bow in gratitude. [Bell]

Wise elder brother, the teacher Shariputra,
to whom we bow in gratitude. [Bell]

Showing love for parents, the teacher Mahamaudgalyayana,
to whom we bow in gratitude. [Bell]

Master of the Vinaya, the teacher Upali,
to whom we bow in gratitude. [Bell]

Recorder of the teachings, the teacher Ananda,
to whom we bow in gratitude. [Bell]

The first bhikshuni, Mahagotami,
to whom we bow in gratitude. [Bell]

Showing the way fearlessly and compassionately,
the stream of all our Ancestral Teachers,
to whom we bow in gratitude. [Bell]

Sutra Opening Verse

[Bell, Bell, Bell]
Namo Tassa Bhagavato Arahato Samma Sambuddhassa
Namo Tassa Bhagavato Arahato Samma Sambuddhassa
Namo Tassa Bhagavato Arahato Samma Sambuddhassa [Bell]

The Dharma is deep and lovely.
We now have a chance to see, study, and practice it.
We vow to realize its true meaning. [Bell]

The Heart of Perfect Understanding

The bodhisattva Avalokita,
while moving in the deep course of Perfect Understanding,
shed light on the Five Skandhas and found them equally empty.
After this penetration, he overcame ill-being. [Bell]

Listen Shariputra,

form is emptiness and emptiness is form.

Form is not other than emptiness, emptiness is not other than form.

The same is true with feelings, perceptions, mental formations,

and consciousness. [Bell]

Listen Shariputra,

all dharmas are marked with emptiness.

They are neither produced nor destroyed,

neither defiled nor immaculate,

neither increasing nor decreasing.

Therefore in emptiness there is neither form, nor feelings,

nor perceptions, nor mental formations, nor consciousness.

No eye, or ear, or nose, or tongue, or body, or mind.

No form, no sound, no smell, no taste, no touch, no object

of mind.

No realms of elements (from eyes to mind consciousness),

no interdependent origins and no extinction of them (from

ignorance to death and decay).

No ill-being, no cause of ill-being, no end of ill-being, and

no path.

No understanding and no attainment. [Bell]

Because there is no attainment,

the Bodhisattvas, grounded in Perfect Understanding,

find no obstacles for their minds.

Having no obstacles they overcome fear,

liberating themselves forever from illusion, realizing perfect nirvana.

All Buddhas in the past, present, and future,
thanks to this Perfect Understanding,
arrive at full, right, and universal enlightenment. [Bell]

Therefore one should know
that Perfect Understanding is the highest mantra,
  the unequaled mantra,
the destroyer of ill-being, the incorruptible truth.
A mantra of Prajñaparamita should therefore be proclaimed:

Gate gate paragate parasamgate bodhi svaha
Gate gate paragate parasamgate bodhi svaha
Gate gate paragate parasamgate bodhi svaha
[Bell, Bell]

Guided Meditations (1–17)

Closing the Ceremony

PROTECTING AND TRANSFORMING

We, your disciples, who from beginningless time
have made ourselves unhappy out of confusion and ignorance,
being born and dying with no direction,
have now found confidence in the highest awakening.

However much we may have drifted on the ocean of suffering,
today we see clearly that there is a beautiful path.

We turn toward the light of loving kindness to direct us.
We bow deeply to the Awakened One and to our spiritual ancestors
who light up the path before us, guiding every step. [Bell]

The wrongdoings and sufferings that imprison us
are brought about by craving, hatred, ignorance, and pride.
Today we begin anew to purify and free our hearts.
With awakened wisdom, bright as the sun and the full moon,
and immeasurable compassion to help humankind,
we resolve to live beautifully.
With all our heart, we go for refuge to the Three Precious Jewels.
With the boat of loving kindness,
we cross over the ocean of suffering.
With the light of wisdom, we leave behind the forest
    of confusion.
With determination, we learn, reflect, and practice.
Right View is the ground of our actions, in body, speech,
    and mind.
Right Mindfulness embraces us,
walking, standing, lying down, and sitting,
speaking, smiling, coming in, and going out.
Whenever anger or anxiety enter our heart,
we are determined to breathe mindfully and come back to ourselves.
With every step, we will walk within the Pure Land.
With every look, the Dharmakaya is revealed.
We are careful and attentive as sense organs touch sense objects
so mindfulness will protect us all day,
so all habit energies can be observed and easily transformed. [Bell]

May our heart's garden of awakening
bloom with hundreds of flowers.
May we bring the feelings of peace and joy into every
household.
May we plant wholesome seeds on the ten thousand paths.
May we never have the need to leave the Sangha body.
May we never attempt to escape the suffering of the world,
always being present wherever beings need our help.
May mountains and rivers be our witness in this moment
as we bow our heads and request the Lord of Compassion
to embrace us all. [Bell, Bell]

GATHA FOR BEGINNING ANEW

Due to attachment, anger, and foolishness,
I have committed numberless mistakes
in speech, deed, and thought.
I bow my head and beg to repent.
Wholeheartedly, I ask Buddha to witness
my vow from today to begin anew,
to live day and night in mindfulness,
and not to repeat my previous mistakes.
Homage to the bodhisattva of repentance.
[Bell, Bell, Bell]

All wrongdoing arises from the mind.
When the mind is purified, what trace of wrong is left?
After repentance, my heart is light like the white clouds

that have always floated over the ancient forest in freedom.
[Bell, Bell]

TAKING REFUGE

I take refuge in the Buddha,
the one who shows me the way in this life.
I take refuge in the Dharma,
the way of understanding and of love.
I take refuge in the Sangha,
the community that lives in harmony and awareness. [Bell]

Dwelling in the refuge of Buddha,
I clearly see the path of light and beauty in the world.
Dwelling in the refuge of Dharma,
I learn to open many doors on the path of transformation.
Dwelling in the refuge of Sangha,
shining light that supports me, keeping my practice free of
    obstruction. [Bell]

Taking refuge in the Buddha in myself,
I aspire to help all people recognize their own awakened nature,
realizing the mind of love.
Taking refuge in the Dharma in myself,
I aspire to help all people fully master the ways of practice
and walk together on the path of liberation.
Taking refuge in the Sangha in myself,
I aspire to help all people build Fourfold Communities

to embrace all beings and support their transformation.
[Bell, Bell]

SHARING THE MERIT

Reciting the sutras, practicing the way of awareness,
gives rise to benefits without limit.
We vow to share the fruits with all beings.
We vow to offer tribute to parents, teachers, friends, and
    numerous beings
who give guidance and support along the path.
[Bell, Bell, Bell]

CEREMONY 2

{Incense Offering (Version One), Visualization of the Buddha, Touching the Earth, Sutra Opening Verse, The Heart of Perfect Understanding, Guided Meditations 18–33, Refuge Chant, Repentance Gatha, Sharing the Merit}

Opening the Ceremony

INCENSE OFFERING (Version One)

In gratitude, we offer this incense
throughout space and time
to all Buddhas and Bodhisattvas.
May it be fragrant as Earth herself,
reflecting careful efforts,
wholehearted mindfulness,
and the fruit of understanding, slowly ripening.
May we and all beings
be companions of Buddhas and Bodhisattvas.
May we awaken from forgetfulness
and realize our true home. [Bell]

Visualization of the Buddha

The Buddha is a flower of humanity
who practiced the way for countless lives.
He appeared on this Earth
as a prince who left his royal palace
to practice at the foot of the bodhi tree.
He conquered illusion.
When the morning star arose,
he realized a great path of awakening
and turned the wheel of the Dharma.

With one-pointed mind all species aspire to experience the path of
no birth and no death.
With one-pointed mind all species will experience the path of no
birth and no death.

Namo Tassa Bhagavato Arahato Samma Sambuddhassa
Namo Tassa Bhagavato Arahato Samma Sambuddhassa
Namo Tassa Bhagavato Arahato Samma Sambuddhassa [Bell]

Touching the Earth

Offering light in the Ten Directions,
the Buddha, the Dharma, and the Sangha,
to whom we bow in gratitude. [Bell]

Teaching and living the way of awareness
in the very midst of suffering and confusion,
Shakyamuni Buddha, the Fully Enlightened One,
to whom we bow in gratitude. [Bell]

Cutting through ignorance, awakening our hearts and our minds,
Manjushri, the Bodhisattva of Great Understanding,
to whom we bow in gratitude. [Bell]

Working mindfully, working joyfully for the sake of all beings,
Samantabhadra, the Bodhisattva of Great Action,
to whom we bow in gratitude. [Bell]

Listening deeply, serving beings in countless ways,
Avalokiteshvara, the Bodhisattva of Great Compassion,
to whom we bow in gratitude. [Bell]

Fearless and persevering through realms of suffering and
    darkness,
Kshitigarbha, the Bodhisattva of Great Aspiration,
to whom we bow in gratitude. [Bell]

Seed of awakening and loving kindness
in children and all beings,
Maitreya, the Buddha to-be-born,
to whom we bow in gratitude. [Bell]

Convener of the Sangha, the teacher Mahakashyapa,
To whom we bow in gratitude. [Bell]

Wise elder brother, the teacher Shariputra,
To whom we bow in gratitude. [Bell]

Showing love for parents, the teacher Mahamaudgalyayana,
To whom we bow in gratitude. [Bell]

Master of the Vinaya, the teacher Upali,
To whom we bow in gratitude. [Bell]

Recorder of the teachings, the teacher Ananda,
To whom we bow in gratitude. [Bell]

The first bhikshuni, Mahagotami,
To whom we bow in gratitude. [Bell]

Showing the way fearlessly and compassionately,
the stream of all our Ancestral Teachers,
to whom we bow in gratitude. [Bell]

Sutra Opening Verse

[Bell, Bell, Bell]
Namo Tassa Bhagavato Arahato Samma Sambuddhassa
Namo Tassa Bhagavato Arahato Samma Sambuddhassa
Namo Tassa Bhagavato Arahato Samma Sambuddhassa [Bell]

The Dharma is deep and lovely
We now have a chance to see, study, and practice it.
We vow to realize its true meaning. [Bell]

THE HEART OF PERFECT UNDERSTANDING

The bodhisattva Avalokita,
while moving in the deep course of Perfect Understanding,
shed light on the five skandhas and found them equally empty.
After this penetration, he overcame ill-being. [Bell]

Listen Shariputra,
form is emptiness and emptiness is form.
Form is not other than emptiness, emptiness is not other than form.
The same is true with feelings, perceptions, mental formations, and
     consciousness. [Bell]

Listen Shariputra,
all dharmas are marked with emptiness.
They are neither produced nor destroyed,
neither defiled nor immaculate,
neither increasing nor decreasing.
Therefore in emptiness there is neither form, nor feelings,
nor perceptions, nor mental formations, nor consciousness.
No eye, or ear, or nose, or tongue, or body, or mind.
No form, no sound, no smell, no taste, no touch, no object of mind.
No realms of elements (from eyes to mind consciousness),
no interdependent origins and no extinction of them (from ignorance
     to death and decay).
No ill-being, no cause of ill-being, no end of ill-being, and
     no path.
No understanding and no attainment. [Bell]

Because there is no attainment,
the Bodhisattvas, grounded in Perfect Understanding,
find no obstacles for their minds.
Having no obstacles, they overcome fear,
liberating themselves forever from illusion, realizing perfect nirvana.
All Buddhas in the past, present, and future,
thanks to this Perfect Understanding,
arrive at full, right, and universal enlightenment. [Bell]

Therefore one should know
that Perfect Understanding is the highest mantra,
the unequaled mantra,
the destroyer of ill–being, the incorruptible truth.
A mantra of Prajñaparamita should therefore be proclaimed:

Gate gate paragate parasamgate bodhi svaha
Gate gate paragate parasamgate bodhi svaha
Gate gate paragate parasamgate bodhi svaha
[Bell, Bell]

Guided Meditations (18–33)

Closing the Ceremony

THE REFUGE CHANT

Incense perfumes the atmosphere.
A lotus blooms and the Buddha appears.

The world of suffering and discrimination
is filled with the light of the rising sun.
As the dust of fear and anxiety settles,
with open heart, one-pointed mind
I turn to the Three Jewels. [Bell]

The Fully Enlightened One, beautifully seated, peaceful and smiling,
a living source of understanding and compassion,
to the Buddha I go for refuge. [Bell]

The path of mindful living,
leading to healing, joy, and enlightenment, the way of peace,
to the Dharma I go for refuge. [Bell]

The loving and supportive community of practice,
realizing harmony, awareness, and liberation,
to the Sangha I go for refuge. [Bell]

I am aware that the Three Gems are within my heart.
I vow to realize them,
practicing mindful breathing and smiling,
looking deeply into things.
I vow to understand living beings and their suffering.
I vow to cultivate compassion and loving kindness,
to practice joy and equanimity. [Bell]

I vow to offer joy to one person in the morning,
to help relieve the grief of one person in the afternoon.

Living simply and sanely with few possessions,
keeping my body healthy.
I vow to let go of all worries and anxiety
in order to be light and free. [Bell]

I am aware that I owe so much
to my parents, teachers, friends, and all beings.
I vow to be worthy of their trust, to practice wholeheartedly
so that understanding and compassion will flower,
helping living beings be free from their suffering.
May the Buddha, the Dharma, and the Sangha
support my efforts.
[Bell, Bell]

REPENTANCE GATHA

Due to attachment, anger, and foolishness,
I have committed numberless mistakes
in speech, deed, and thought.
I bow my head and beg to repent.
Wholeheartedly, I ask Buddha to witness
my vow from today to begin anew,
to live day and night in mindfulness,
and not to repeat my previous mistakes.

Homage to the bodhisattva of repentance.
[Bell, Bell, Bell]

All wrongdoing arises from the mind.
When the mind is purified, what trace of wrong is left?
After repentance, my heart is light like the white clouds
that have always floated over the ancient forest in freedom.
[Bell, Bell]

SHARING THE MERIT

Reciting the sutras, practicing the way of awareness
gives rise to benefit without limit.
We vow to share the fruits with all beings.
We vow to offer tribute to parents, teachers, friends, and numerous
    beings
who give guidance and support along the path.
[Bell, Bell, Bell]

CEREMONY 3

{Incense Offering (Version One), Visualization of the Buddha, Touching the Earth, Sutra Opening Verse, The Heart of Perfect Understanding, Guided Meditations 34–46, Turning to the Tathagata, Repentance Gatha, Taking Refuge, Sharing the Merit}

Opening the Ceremony

INCENSE OFFERING (Version One)

In gratitude, we offer this incense
throughout space and time
to all Buddhas and Bodhisattvas.
May it be fragrant as Earth herself,
reflecting careful efforts,
wholehearted awareness,
and the fruit of understanding, slowly ripening.
May we and all beings
be companions of Buddhas and Bodhisattvas.
May we awaken from forgetfulness
and realize our true home. [Bell]

VISUALIZATION OF THE BUDDHA

The countenance of the Buddha is as beautiful as the moon.
The three worlds praise the World-Honored One
who is able to subdue all obstacles
and who is admired by gods and humans.
Homage to Shakyamuni Buddha, my root teacher. [Bell]

TOUCHING THE EARTH

Opening Gatha

The one who bows and the one who is bowed to
are both, by nature, empty.
Therefore the communication between them
is inexpressibly perfect.
Our practice center is the Net of Indra
reflecting all Buddhas everywhere.
And with my person in front of each Buddha,
I go with my whole life for refuge. [Bell]

Prostrations

Offering light in the Ten Directions,
the Buddha, the Dharma, and the Sangha,
to whom we bow in gratitude. [Bell]

Teaching and living the way of awareness
in the very midst of suffering and confusion,

Shakyamuni Buddha, the Fully Enlightened One,
to whom we bow in gratitude. [Bell]

Cutting through ignorance, awakening our hearts and our minds,
Manjushri, the Bodhisattva of Great Understanding,
to whom we bow in gratitude. [Bell]

Working mindfully, working joyfully for the sake of all beings,
Samantabhadra, the Bodhisattva of Great Action,
to whom we bow in gratitude. [Bell]

Listening deeply, serving beings in countless ways,
Avalokiteshvara, the Bodhisattva of Great Compassion,
to whom we bow in gratitude. [Bell]

Fearless and persevering through realms of suffering and darkness,
Kshitigarbha, the Bodhisattva of Great Aspiration,
to whom we bow in gratitude. [Bell]

Seed of awakening and loving kindness in children and all beings,
Maitreya, the Buddha to–be–born,
To whom we bow in gratitude. [Bell]

Convener of the Sangha, the teacher Mahakashyapa,
to whom we bow in gratitude. [Bell]

Wise elder brother, the teacher Shariputra,
to whom we bow in gratitude. [Bell]

Showing love for parents, the teacher Mahamaudgalyayana,
to whom we bow in gratitude. [Bell]

Master of the Vinaya, the teacher Upali,
to whom we bow in gratitude. [Bell]

Recorder of the teachings, the teacher Ananda,
to whom we bow in gratitude. [Bell]

The first bhikshuni, Mahagotami,
to whom we bow in gratitude. [Bell]

Showing the way fearlessly and compassionately,
the stream of all our Ancestral Teachers,
to whom we bow in gratitude. [Bell]

SUTRA OPENING VERSE

[Bell, Bell, Bell]
Namo Tassa Bhagavato Arahato Samma Sambuddhassa
Namo Tassa Bhagavato Arahato Samma Sambuddhassa
Namo Tassa Bhagavato Arahato Samma Sambuddhassa [Bell]

The Dharma is deep and lovely.
We now have a chance to see, study, and practice it.
We vow to realize its true meaning. [Bell]

THE HEART OF PERFECT UNDERSTANDING

The bodhisattva Avalokita,
while moving in the deep course of Perfect Understanding,
shed light on the Five Skandhas and found them equally empty.
After this penetration he overcame ill-being. [Bell]

Listen Shariputra,
form is emptiness and emptiness is form.
Form is not other than emptiness, emptiness is not other than form.
The same is true with feelings, perceptions, mental formations,
    and consciousness. [Bell]

Listen Shariputra,
all dharmas are marked with emptiness.
They are neither produced nor destroyed,
neither defiled nor immaculate,
neither increasing nor decreasing.
Therefore in emptiness there is neither form, nor feelings,
nor perceptions, nor mental formations, nor consciousness.
No eye, or ear, or nose, or tongue, or body, or mind.
No form, no sound, no smell, no taste, no touch, no object of mind.
No realms of elements (from eyes to mind consciousness),
no interdependent origins and no extinction of them,
(from ignorance to death and decay).
No ill-being, no cause of ill-being, no end of ill-being and no path.
No understanding and no attainment. [Bell]

Because there is no attainment,
the Bodhisattvas, grounded in Perfect Understanding,
find no obstacles for their minds.
Having no obstacles they overcome fear,
liberating themselves forever from illusion, realizing perfect nirvana.
All Buddhas in the past, present, and future,
thanks to this perfect understanding,
arrive at full, right, and universal enlightenment. [Bell]

Therefore one should know
that Perfect Understanding is the highest mantra,
the unequaled mantra,
the destroyer of ill-being, the incorruptible truth.
A mantra of Prajñaparamita should therefore be proclaimed:

Gate gate paragate parasamgate bodhi svaha
Gate gate paragate parasamgate bodhi svaha
Gate gate paragate parasamgate bodhi svaha
[Bell, Bell]

Guided Meditations (34–46)

Closing the Ceremony

TURNING TO THE TATHAGATA

I touch the earth deeply, turning to the Tathagata,
the lighthouse that shines over the ocean of dust and suffering.

Lord of Compassion, embrace us with your love,
for today we are determined to return to our true home. [Bell]

We, your spiritual children, still owe so much gratitude
to our parents, teachers, friends, and all other beings.
Looking over the Three Realms and across the Four Quarters,
we see all species drowning in an ocean of misfortune.
It wakes us with a start.
Although we have turned in the right direction,
the shore of awakening still lies very far away.
Fortunately, we see the hands of the Compassionate One
bringing relief to every corner of the world. [Bell]

With one-pointed mind, we return, taking refuge.
We aspire to be the spiritual children of the Tathagata.
We unify our body and mind before the Buddha's throne,
releasing all attachment and negativity.
With great respect, we now aspire to receive the wonderful teachings.
We shall always practice diligently and carefully,
our mindfulness trainings and concentration nourished to maturity,
for the fruit of understanding to be ripened in the future.
We ask the bodhisattvas to protect us day and night.
May the Buddha, Dharma, and Sangha show us their compassion.
   [Bell]

We know that the fruits of our past actions are still heavy,
that the merit from our virtues is still frail,
that we are often full of wrong perceptions,

that our capacity to understand is poor,
that the impurities of our mind still arise very easily,
that our practices of listening and contemplation are not firm.
In this moment we entrust ourselves to the Lotus Throne,
and, with our five limbs laid gently on the earth, we now pray.
Infinite loving kindness, please expand and envelop us
so that we too may open our hearts. [Bell]

We, your spiritual children for countless past lives,
have chased after worldly things,
unable to recognize the clear, pure basis of our True Mind.
Our actions of body, speech, and mind have been unwholesome.
We have drowned in ignorant cravings, jealousy, hatred, and anger.
But now the sound of the great bell has caused us to awaken
with a heart that is determined to renew our body and our mind.
Please help us completely remove the red dust of all
wrongdoings, mistakes, and faults. [Bell]

We, your spiritual children in this moment,
make the vow to leave all our habit energies behind,
and for the whole of our life to go for refuge to the Sangha.
Awakened One, please place your hand over us in protection,
so that loving kindness and compassion will guide and assist us.
We promise that when we practice meditation,
when we take part in Dharma discussion,
when we stand, walk, lie, or sit,
when we cook, wash, work, or play,
when we recite the names of the Buddhas and Bodhisattvas,

when we offer incense or when we touch the earth,
every step will bring peace and joy to the world,
every smile will be resplendent with freedom.
We will live mindfully in each and every moment
to demonstrate the way of liberation from suffering.
We vow to touch the Pure Land with every step.
We promise in every contact
to be in touch with the ultimate dimension,
taking steps on the soil of reality, breathing the air of true
    emptiness,
lighting up wisdom to make resplendent the wonderful
    True Mind,
drawing aside the dark curtain of ignorance,
with our body and mind peaceful and happy,
free and at leisure until the moment when we leave this life,
our heart with no regrets, our body without pain,
our thoughts unclouded by ignorance,
our mindfulness clear and bright, and our six senses calm
as when entering meditative concentration. [Bell]

If necessary to be reborn, we will always do so
as the spiritual children of the Tathagata.
We will continue in the work of helping other beings,
bringing them all over to the shore of awakening.
Realizing the Three Bodies and the Four Wisdoms,
using the Five Eyes and the Six Miracles,
manifesting thousands of appropriate forms,
being present at one time in all the Three Worlds,

coming in and going out in freedom and with ease,
we will not abandon anyone, helping all beings to transform,
bringing all to the shore of no regression. [Bell]

Space is without limit. There are infinite living beings,
and the same is true with afflictions and results of past actions.
We pray that our aspirations will also become infinite.
We bow to the Awakened One as we make this vow.
We will maintain virtue, sharing the merit with countless others
in order to fully repay the gratitude that we owe
and to teach the practice everywhere within the Three Realms.
May we, alongside all species of living beings,
fully realize the Great Awakened Understanding.
[Bell, Bell]

REPENTANCE GATHA

Due to attachment, anger, and foolishness,
I have committed numberless mistakes
in speech, deed, and thought.
I bow my head and beg to repent.
Wholeheartedly, I ask Buddha to witness
my vow from today to begin anew,
to live day and night in mindfulness,
and not to repeat my previous mistakes.
Homage to the bodhisattva of repentance.
[Bell, Bell, Bell]

All wrongdoing arises from the mind.
When the mind is purified, what trace of wrong is left?
After repentance, my heart is light like the white clouds
that have always floated over the ancient forest in freedom.
[Bell, Bell]

TAKING REFUGE

I take refuge in the Buddha,
the one who shows me the way in this life.
I take refuge in the Dharma,
the way of understanding and of love.
I take refuge in the Sangha,
the community that lives in harmony and awareness. [Bell]

Dwelling in the refuge of Buddha,
I clearly see the path of light and beauty in the world.
Dwelling in the refuge of Dharma,
I learn to open many doors on the path of transformation.
Dwelling in the refuge of Sangha,
shining light that supports me, keeping my practice free of
     obstruction. [Bell]

Taking refuge in the Buddha in myself,
I aspire to help all people recognize their own awakened nature,
realizing the mind of love.
Taking refuge in the Dharma in myself,
I aspire to help all people fully master the ways of practice

and walk together on the path of liberation.
Taking refuge in the Sangha in myself,
I aspire to help all people build Fourfold Communities
to embrace all beings and support their transformation.
[Bell, Bell]

SHARING THE MERIT

Reciting the sutras, practicing the way of awareness,
gives rise to benefits without limit.
We vow to share the fruits with all beings.
We vow to offer tribute to parents, teachers, friends, and numerous
    beings
who give guidance and support along the path.
[Bell, Bell, Bell]

Glossary

Ananda   Cousin and disciple of the Buddha, and his attendant for many years, who could recall by heart all the Buddha's discourses.

Avalokiteshvara   Bodhisattva of Great Compassion and Deep Listening who is able to hear the cries of the world and relieve the suffering of living beings.

Avatamsaka Sutra (Flower Ornament Sutra)   A Mahayana sutra of the third century C.E. Two main ideas it contains are aimlessness and interbeing. Aimlessness refers to the idea that we already have everything we are looking for; we already are what we want to become. Be yourself, life is precious as it is, all the elements for your happiness are already there. Interbeing and interpenetration show us that when we look deeply into any one thing we see that everything else is contained in it, and also that it is contained in everything else. The one contains the all, and the all contains the one.

Bamboo Grove   Site of the Buddha's first monastery, located near Rajagriha, capital of the Kingdom of Magadha, and offered to the Buddha by King Bimbisara.

Bodhicitta   A Sanskrit term that means literally "the mind of awakening." Our bodhicitta, our mind of love, or mind of awakening, is the deep wish to cultivate understanding in ourselves in order to bring happiness to many beings. It is the motivating force for the practice of mindful living.

Bodhisattva   Literally "enlightened being," one committed to enlightening oneself and others so that all may be liberated from suffering.

Dharanimdhara   Earth Holder bodhisattva from the Lotus Sutra who represents our capacity to protect the Earth.

Dipankara   The first of the twenty-four Buddhas preceding the historical Buddha who symbolizes all the Buddhas of the past. Buddha Dipankara was the teacher of Shakyamuni Buddha in the past and predicted his enlightenment in this lifetime.

Drsta dharma sukha viharin   The expression in Sanskrit meaning "dwelling happily in the present moment."

Eightfold Path   The path to well-being (the fourth Noble Truth): Right View, Right Thinking, Right Speech, Right Action, Right Livelihood, Right Effort, Right Mindfulness, and Right Concentration.

Five Faculties and Five Powers   Faith, diligence, mindfulness, concentration, and insight. These five energies are called Faculties when they are in the process of development to help us practice, and are called Powers when they have the strength to radiate to all those around us. They are the only kind of power that a true practitioner wishes to possess.

Four Noble Truths   Suffering, the origin of suffering, the cessation of suffering, the path that leads to the cessation of suffering, that is, the Noble Eightfold Path.

Fourfold Sangha   The Sangha of monks, nuns, laymen, and laywomen.

Jeta Grove   Site of a monastery where the Buddha spent much time and passed many rainy retreats. Located in the Eastern Park near Shravasti, capital of the Kingdom of Koshala, it was purchased for the Buddha by his lay student, the generous merchant Anathapindika.

Kapilavastu   Capital of the Kingdom of Shakya, where Siddhartha lived with his family in the royal palace before he left to practice asceticism.

Kashyapa   The sixth of the seven Buddhas of antiquity.

Konakamuni   The fifth of the seven Buddhas of antiquity.

Krakkucchandha   The fourth of the seven Buddhas of antiquity.

Kshitigarbha   Earth Store bodhisattva who vows to save beings in the realms of greatest suffering.

Kshitigarbha Sutra   A Mahayana sutra in the Chinese Canon, it originated in Central Asia and was translated from Sanskrit into Chinese. It describes the past lives of the bodhisattva Kshitigarbha, his vow and practices, and the benefits that come to those who pay homage to him.

Mahagotami Sister of Maya and stepmother of Siddhartha, who raised Siddhartha after the passing away of his mother. She was the first woman to be ordained a bhikshuni in the Buddha's Sangha.

Mahakaccayana A great disciple of the Buddha, known for explaining short statements of the Buddha.

Mahakashyapa Mahakashyapa, also known just as Kashyapa, was a disciple of the Buddha who smiled when the Buddha held up a flower, received the "mind seal" of transmission from the Buddha, and later was acknowledged as the "leader of the Sangha" after the Buddha entered nirvana.

Mahamaudgalyayana A great disciple of the Buddha, known for his clear and powerful mind and for his loyalty to his mother. He was Shariputra's boyhood friend and they joined the Buddha's Sangha together.

Maitreya The Buddha of the future, succeeding Shakyamuni. Perhaps the Buddha-to-be-born may come in the form of Sangha, rather than as an individual.

Manjushri Bodhisattva of Great Understanding who is able to cut through the bonds of ignorance and see things clearly as they are.

Maya Wife of Suddhodana, mother of Siddhartha, who died seven days after his birth.

Mindful manners (or fine manners) A set of guidelines for living daily life in the monastery with mindfulness. Together with the Ten Novice Precepts and the gathas for daily living, the fine manners form the basic study and practice of novice monks and nuns.

Nagapushpa Assembly The assembly that gathers around the Dragon Flower Tree to hear the teachings of Maitreya, the Buddha-to-be.

Nihilism The belief that we become nothing when we die.

Nirvana The ultimate freedom from all notions.

Original Sangha The community of practitioners living with and at the time of the historical Buddha, Shakyamuni.

Permanence The belief, whether conscious or unconscious, that we will live forever.

Prabhutaratna Also known as Buddha Many Jewels. The Buddha of the Ultimate Dimension introduced by Shakyamuni Buddha while delivering the Lotus Sutra.

Prasenajit King of Koshala, of which Shravasti was the capital. He was a friend and lay disciple of the Buddha.

Pure Land Mahayana Buddhism speaks of a Pure Land in the west presided over by Amitabha Buddha. Pure Land practitioners believe that when they die they will be reborn in the Pure Land. But, as with the kingdom of God, we can be in touch with the Pure Land here and now. Through our practice of mindful breathing and walking, wherever we are becomes the Pure Land.

Purna One of the great disciples of the Buddha, known for his ability to teach the Dharma and his willingness to go to a difficult place to teach.

Rahula The biological son of the Buddha became a monk after his father. He is known as having mastery of the "secret teachings." This refers to his way of not outwardly showing his deep understanding and insight.

Sadaparibhuta Also known as Bodhisattva Never Despising. A bodhisattva who never gives up on anyone as he is able to see and tell people of their capacity to awaken, their Buddha nature. His name also means "showing constant respect."

Samadhi Concentration, a state of deep focus and absorption.

Samantabhadra Bodhisattva of wise and compassionate action, who made the ten great vows of practice found in the Avatamsaka Sutra.

Samsara The cycle of birth and death in which one does not find the path of awakening, love, and understanding. In samsara you are caught in your suffering without a clear direction for your life.

Seven Elements of Enlightenment Also called the Seven Limbs of Awakening, they are: mindfulness, concentration, investigation of phenomena, diligence, letting go, ease, and joy.

Shakyamuni Name referring to the historical Buddha, meaning literally "sage of the Shakya clan." Shakya is Siddhartha's family name. Muni in Sanskrit means ascetic; monk; silent one.

Shariputra A great disciple of the Buddha, brilliant and capable; he was a wise elder brother to all in the Buddha's Sangha.

Shikhin The second of the seven Buddhas of antiquity.

Six Harmonies (Sanskrit: *sharaniya-dharma***)** The six practices taught by the Buddha for maintaining harmony in the Sangha. They are: the harmony of body, speech, thoughts, precepts, sharing benefits, and views.

Six Paramitas, or Perfections The six practices of a bodhisattva: giving, mindfulness trainings, inclusiveness, diligence, meditation, wisdom.

Skandha The five skandhas (aggregates) are the elements that make up each person, including the body (form), feelings, perceptions, mental formations, and consciousness.

Subhuti A great disciple of the Buddha, known for his insight into emptiness. He appears in Mahayana sutras as an open and inquiring student of the Dharma.

Suddhodana King of the Kingdom of Shakya. Father of Prince Siddhartha.

Tathagata "The one who comes from suchness and the one who goes to suchness" is a name the Buddha used for himself.

Upali Vinaya Master of the Buddha's Sangha.

Vipashyin The first of the seven former Buddhas.

Vishvabhu The third of the seven Buddhas of antiquity.

Vulture Peak Gridhrakuta Mountain, near the town of Rajagriha in the Kingdom of Magadha, where the Buddha sometimes stayed and taught.

Parallax Press, a nonprofit organization, publishes books on engaged Buddhism and the practice of mindfulness by Thich Nhat Hanh and other authors. All of Thich Nhat Hanh's work is available at our online store and in our free catalog. For a copy of the catalog, please contact:

Parallax Press
P.O. Box 7355, Berkeley, CA 94707
Tel: (510) 525-0101 • www.parallax.org

Monastics and laypeople practice the art of mindful living in the tradition of Thich Nhat Hanh at retreat communities in France and the United States. To reach any of these communities, or for information about individuals and families joining for a practice period, please contact:

Plum Village
13 Martineau
33580 Dieulivol, France
www.plumvillage.org

Blue Cliff Monastery
3 Mindfulness Road
Pine Bush, NY 12566
www.bluecliffmonastery.org

Deer Park Monastery
2499 Melru Lane
Escondido, CA 92026
www.deerparkmonastery.org

For a worldwide directory of Sanghas practicing in the tradition of Thich Nhat Hanh, please visit www.iamhome.org